P9-DTE-240

BOSWELLIAN STUDIES

Thou art a Retailer of Phrases;
And dost deal in Remnants of Remnants,
Like a Maker of Pincushions.

Congreve's Way of the World,

Boswellian Studies

A BIBLIOGRAPHY

ANTHONY E. BROWN

Second Edition, Revised

ARCHON BOOKS

1972

First edition published 1964 in Cairo. This revised and expanded
edition published 1972 by Archon Books, The Shoe String Press,
Inc., Hamden, Connecticut 06514. © 1972 by The Shoe String
Press, Inc. All rights reserved. Printed in the United States of
America.
Library of Congress catalog card number 75-155892
International standard book number 0-208-01214-1

For
Four Named Helen

Contents

Foreword

In revising my catalog of the critical approaches to James Boswell and his work, I have retained the original format and numbering system and I have enumerated the new items through the use of decimals, which provides the greatest flexibility for future revisions. The subject index has been completely reworked to accommodate the additions.

Since the time this list first appeared in 1964 in a publication in Egypt, I have intensified my searches, especially in Boswell's contemporary period and in the years since 1964, the result being an addition of over a hundred new items for the General Studies section and a large number of reviews of early editions and of such new materials as Pottle's account of Boswell's early career (Item 41.1) and Marshall Waingrow's edition of the correspondence surrounding the writing and publication of *The Life of Johnson* (Item 28.2).

The revision and expansion of this list has been considerably aided by the observations offered me by many of the Boswell-Johnson students who made use of the first edition and freely gave me the advantage of their knowledge in the field. I have silently incorporated their emendations and additions, and, together with the corrections I have made, their help has increased the value of my work.

A. E. B.

Abbreviations

Atlantic Mo.	Atlantic Monthly	*NYTBR*	New York Times Book Review
Biblio. NQ	Bibliographical Notes and Queries	*NQ*	Notes and Queries
BNYPL	Bulletin of the New York Public Library	*PMLA*	Publications of the Modern Language Association
CE	College English		
Church QR	Church Quarterly Review	*PQ*	Philological Quarterly
CLAJ	College Language Association Journal	*PULC*	Princeton University Library Chronicle
ELH	Journal of English Literary History	*Pub. Weekly*	Publisher's Weekly
HLN	Harvard Library Notes	*QQR*	Queen's Quarterly Review
JRLB	John Rylands Library Bulletin	*QR*	Quarterly Review
		RES	Review of English Studies
JEGP	Journal of English and Germanic Philology	*Rev.*	Review
		SAQ	South Atlantic Quarterly
LAR	Library Association Record	*SEL*	Studies in English Literature
L Jour	Library Journal	*SP*	Studies in Philology
MLF	Modern Language Forum		
MLN	Modern Language Notes	*SRL*	Saturday Review of Literature
MLQ	Modern Language Quarterly	*TLS*	London Times Literary Supplement
MLR	Modern Language Review	*UTQ*	University of Toronto Quarterly
MP	Modern Philology	*VQR*	Virginia Quarterly Review
Nat. Rev.	National Review		
NCR	New Century Review	*YULG*	Yale University Library Gazette
New Repub.	New Republic		
NYHTBR	New York Herald Tribune Book Review		

Introduction

In preparing a catalog of the critical writing on James Boswell and his work, I have attempted to organize into a single instrument as much material as my research has been able to bring to light. Undoubtedly, there are omissions, especially from that formidable forest of Nineteenth-Century periodicals through the shadows of whose pages the paths are not carefully marked. I have struggled to obtain all the information possible about each entry, but in some cases partial coverage was all that could be accomplished.

As for the choice of primary works, I have not attempted to list every edition of Boswell's writing; Professor Pottle has already compiled such a catalog in his 1929 *Literary Career of James Boswell*. I have, however, listed some of the first editions of Boswell's work, especially when abundant critical material on those editions became evident, and I have included those editions that have appeared since Pottle's bibliography was published, the significant editions of *The Life of Johnson*, and other materials with reviews when they could be located. It should be understood that in the work at Yale some of the editions of the journals have been published in England by William Heinemann; these volumes do not always coincide precisely with the McGraw-Hill editions, the Heinemann journals often being printed a year following the McGraw-Hill ones and on different plates in some printings with some changes in format, introductory matter, illustrations, and pagination. Thus, the reader should be aware of variations that may occur when the different texts are cited.

The third section of the bibliography, "The Boswell Papers," consists of all the material that I could identify as specifically related to the discoveries, purchases, processing, and publication to date of the Malahide-Fettercairn manusctipts and other papers by the Yale committee. It is likely that some of the entries in the fourth section, "General Studies," might be included in the third, for some authors have chosen to begin their articles with the finding of the private papers and have launched forth onto the broader fields of Boswelliana. Some items inaccessible to me I have listed according to inferences I could make from the titles or from the sort of periodicals in which they appeared.

The fourth section contains everything available to my research through the sources at my disposal, from scholarly interpretation to whimsical sketch. I have annotated as many of the entries as possible, but when the title of an entry makes clear the matter it concerns, I frequently have not added a note.

I should like to repeat my acknowledgements of indebtedness to Dr. James L. Clifford, of Columbia University, whose personal attentions to my work provided much of its accuracy and many of its entries, and to Professor Frederick A. Pottle, of Yale, who opened to my use the vast experience he has gained in the field. Many of his suggestions concerning format, pertinent information, and additional entries are evident in this work. Very special gratitude is extended to Dr. John M. Aden, my professor at Vanderbilt University, whose kind strictness, patience, and insistence upon technical proprieties inspired the original of this work and prompted the present expanded version.

Western Carolina University   A. E. B.
Cullowhee, North Carolina

SECTION ONE
Editions

Section One
Editions

A. BOSWELL'S JOURNALS

1. SCOTT, Geoffrey, and Frederick A. Pottle (eds.). *The Private Papers of James Boswell from Malahide Castle in the Collection of Lieutenant Colonel Ralph Heyward Isham.* 18 vols. Mount Vernon, N. Y.: Privately Printed by Rudge, 1928-1934. Scott edited vols. 1-6; Pottle, vols. 7-18 of the 570 copy limited edition. Vols. 1-3 reviewed by Pottle, F. A. *SRL*, V (Feb. 16, 1929), 677-678.

2. POTTLE, F. A., Joseph Foladare, John P. Kirby, and Others (eds.). *Index to the Private Papers of James Boswell from Malahide Castle in the Collection of Lieutenant Colonel Ralph Heyward Isham.* London and New York: Oxford University Press, 1937.

3. *Boswell's London Journal, 1762-1763,* ed. F. A. Pottle, with a Preface by Christopher Morley. New York: McGraw-Hill, 1950; London: William Heinemann, 1950 (American plates used); London: William Heinemann, 1951: a limited edition, reset entirely, with extra illustrations, containing in addition Boswell's "Journal of My Jaunt, Harvest, 1762" and a publisher's note in place of Morley's Preface. Pottle's important "History of the Boswell Papers" is included in the 1951 Heinemann edition. See item 429 for portions of Morley's Preface. Record collectors may obtain excerpts read by Anthony Quayle on Caedmon Records, TC1093.
    Reviews: (a) Abbott, C. C., *Listener*, XLII (Dec. 28, 1950), 843-844; (b) Auden, W. H., *New Yorker*, XXVI (Nov. 25, 1950), 146-148; (c) Bacon,

L., *SRL*, XXXIII (Nov. 4, 1950), 11-12; (d) *Booklist*, XLVII (Dec. 1, 1950), 135; (e) Brain, R., *Adelphi*, XXVII (1951), 142-144; (f) Clifford, J. L., *NYTBR*, Nov. 5, 1950, pp. 1, 26; (g) Halsband, R., *Nation*, CLXXI (Nov. 11, 1950), 440-441; (h) Harrison, G. B., *Commonweal*, LIII (Dec. 1, 1950), 205; (i) Kronenberger, L., *Life*, XXX (Jan. 15, 1951), 24; (j) Krutch, J. W., *NYHTBR*, Sept. 5, 1950, pp. 1, 22; (k) Pritchett, V. S., *New Statesman and Nation*, XL (Dec. 9, 1950), 591-592; (l) *Time*, LVI (Nov. 13, 1950), 106, 109-110; (m) *TLS*, Dec. 8, 1950, p. 787; (n) Walbridge, E. F., *L. Jour.*, LXXV (Nov. 1, 1950), 1901.

4. *Boswell in Holland, 1763-1764, and Correspondence with Belle de Zuylen*, ed. F. A. Pottle. New York: McGraw-Hill, 1952; London: William Heinemann, 1952; London: William Heinemann, 1953: limited edition with extra illustrations. Both Heinemann editions were printed from new plates.

Reviews: (a) Bacon, L., *SRL*, XXXV (April 26, 1952), 11; (b) *Booklist*, XLVIII (May 15, 1952), 296; (c) *Catholic World*, CLXXV (Aug., 1952), 399; (d) Dobree, B., *Spectator*, CLXXXVIII (June 6, 1952), 751; (e) Halsband, R., *Hudson Rev.*, V (1952), 443-447; (f) Krutch, J. W., *Nation*, CLXXIV (May 24, 1952), 504-506; (g) Monk, S. H., *New Republic*, CXXVI (May 19, 1952), 18; (h) *New Yorker*, XXVIII (May 10, 1952), 138-139; (i) Quennell, P., *New Statesman and Nation*, XLIV (July 12, 1952), 45-46; (j) Rolo, C. J., *Atlantic Mo.*, CLXXXIX (May, 1952), 77; (k) Shepperson, A. B., *VQR*, XXVIII (1952), 438-441; (l) *TLS*, June 13, 1952, p. 388; (m) Tracy, C., *QQR*, LIX (1952-53), 245-247; (n) Walbridge, E. F., *L. Jour.*, LXXVII (May 1, 1952), 794.

5. *Boswell on the Grand Tour: Germany and Switzer-*

land, 1764, ed. F. A. Pottle. New York: McGraw-Hill, 1953; London: William Heinemann, 1953 (trade edition); London: William Heinemann, 1954 (limited edition).

Reviews: (a) Bacon, L., *SRL,* XXXVI (Nov. 21, 1953), 26-27; (b) Baker, C., *Nation,* CLXXVII (Nov. 14, 1953), 409-410; (c) *Booklist,* L (Nov. 15, 1953), 118; (d) Hopkinson, T., *Spectator,* CXC (Nov. 6, 1953), 514; (e) *New Yorker,* XXIX (Oct. 24, 1953), 160; (f) Pritchett, V. S., *New Statesman and Nation,* XLVI (Oct. 31, 1953), 525-526; (g) Rolo, C. J., *Atlantic Mo.,* CXCII (Nov., 1953), 102; (h) *TLS,* Oct. 30, 1953, p. 694.

6. *Boswell on the Grand Tour: Italy, Corsica, and France 1765-1766,* ed. Frank Brady and F. A. Pottle. New York: McGraw-Hill, 1955; London: William Heinemann, 1956 (limited and trade editions).

Reviews: (a) *Booklist,* LI (June 15, 1955), 423; (b) Fremantle, A., *Reporter,* XII (June 16, 1955), 38-39; (c) Halsband, R., *SRL,* XXXVIII (May 28, 1955), 17; (d) Kolb, G. J., *VQR,* XXXI (Autumn, 1955), 641-644; (e) Litvinoff, E., *Spectator,* CXCV (Oct. 14, 1955), 504; (f) Mayne, R., *New Statesman and Nation,* L (Oct. 15, 1955), 478; (g) *New Yorker,* XXXI (June 11, 1955), 138; (h) Rolo, C. J., *Atlantic Mo.,* CXCV (June 15, 1955), 76; (i) *TLS,* October 7, 1955, p. 590; (j) Walbridge, E. F., *L. Jour.,* LXXX (April 15, 1955), 867.

7. *An Account of Corsica, the Journal of a Tour to that Island; and Memoirs of Pascal Paoli,* by James Boswell. Glasgow: R. and A. Foulis for Edward and Charles Dilly in London, 1768. First Edition.

Reviews: (a) *Critical Rev.,* XXV (March, 1768), 172-181; (b) *Gentleman's Mag.,* XXXVIII (April, 1768), 172-177; (c) *London Mag.,* XXXVII (Feb., 1768), 108-111; (d) *Monthly Rev.,* XXXIX (July, 1768), 43-52; (Aug., 1768), 142-151; (e) *Scots Mag.,* XXX (Feb., 1768), 90-94.

8.   *Journal of a Tour to Corsica; and Memoirs of Pascal Paoli,* by James Boswell, ed. S. C. Roberts. Cambridge University Press, 1923.
Reviews: (a) Birrell, A., *New Statesman,* XXI (July 14, 1923), 417-419; (b) *TLS,* July 5, 1923, p. 453.

9.   _____ , ed. Morchard Bishop. New York: Macmillan, 1952.
Reviews: (a) *Booklist,* XLVIII (July 15, 1952), 380; (b) Breit, H., *NYTBR,* June 8, 1952, p. 25; (c) *New Yorker,* XXVIII (May 17, 1952), 144; (d) *SRL,* XXXV (July 12, 1952), 38.

10.   *Boswell in Search of a Wife, 1766-1769,* ed. Frank Brady and F. A. Pottle. New York: McGraw-Hill, 1956; London: William Heinemann, 1957 (limited and trade editions).
Reviews: (a) Bloom, E. A., *SRL,* XXXIX (Oct. 20, 1956), 21; (b) *Booklist,* LIII (Dec. 1, 1956), 173; (c) Deen, R. F., *Commonweal,* LXV (March 1, 1957), 572; (d) *New Yorker,* XXXII (Nov. 3, 1956), 210-211' (e) Quennell, P., *Spectator,* CXCVI (July 12, 1957), 55-56; (f) Rolo, C. J., *Atlantic Mo.,* CXCVII (Dec., 1956), 94; (g) Squire, J., *Illus. London News,* CCXXXI (Aug. 3, 1957), 187; (h) *Time,* LXVIII (Nov. 26, 1956), 116, 118; (i) *TLS,* July 12, 1957, p. 423.

11.   *Boswell for the Defense, 1769-1774,* ed. W. K. Wimsatt and F. A. Pottle. New York: McGraw-Hill, 1959; London: William Heinemann, 1960.
Reviews: (a) *Booklist,* LVI (Jan. 15, 1960), 291; (b) *Christian Century,* LXXVII (June 8, 1960), 697; (c) Connolly, C., *New Yorker,* XXXV (Jan. 30, 1960), 92-93; 97-98; (d) Lessing, D., *Spectator,* CCV (Oct. 21, 1960), 609-610; (e) Pritchett, V. S., *New Statesman,* LX (Oct. 29, 1960), 663-664; (f) Sutherland, J., *SRL,* XLII (Nov. 28,

1959), 26, 39; (g) *Time*, LXXV (Feb. 1, 1960), 82; (h) *TLS*, Oct. 14, 1960, p. 663; (i) Walbridge, E. F., *L. Jour.*, LXXXV (Jan. 1, 1960), 120.

12.   *The Journal of a Tour to the Hebrides with Samuel Johnson, LL. D.*, by James Boswell. London: Charles Dilly, 1785. First Edition.
Reviews: (a) *Critical Rev.*, LX (Nov., 1785), 337-345; (b) *English Rev.*, VI (Nov., 1785), 370-378; (c) *European Mag.*, VIII (Dec., 1785), 448-452; IX (March, 1786), 168-173; (May, 1786), 340-344; (June, 1786), 413-416; (d) *Gentleman's Mag.*, LV (Nov., 1785), 889-894; (e) *Monthly Rev.*, LXXIV (April, 1786), 277-282; (f) *Scots Mag.*, XLVII (Dec., 1785), 589-595.

13.   *A Journal of a Tour to the Hebrides*, by James Boswell. New York: R. and W. Carr for Inskeep and Bradford, and William McIlhenny, in Boston, 1810; Philadelphia: R. and W. Carr for John F. Watson, 1810. First American Edition.

14.   *Boswell's Journal of a Tour to the Hebrides with Samuel Johnson, LL. D., 1773*, ed. F. A. Pottle and Charles H. Bennett. New York: Viking Press, 1936; London: William Heinemann, 1936. Viking also printed a limited edition of 790 copies in 1936.
Reviews: (a) Bailey, M., *MLN*, LIII (May, 1938), 387-389; (b) Josephson, M., *New Republic*, LXXXIX (Nov. 18, 1936), 80-81; (c) Krutch, J. W., *Nation*, CXLIII (Nov. 7, 1936), 549; (d) Osgood, C. G., *SRL*, XV (Nov. 7, 1936), 5-6; (e) Shepperson, A. B., *VQR*, XIII (Winter, 1937), 143-146; (f) *Time*, XXVIII (Nov. 9, 1936), 79; (g) *TLS*, Nov. 7, 1936, p. 903; (h) Wecter, D., *Yale Rev.*, XXVI (Dec., 1936), 401-404; (i) Wood, F. T., *Englische Studien*, LXXII (Oct., 1937), 120-122.

15. ————. A new Edition. New York: McGraw-Hill, 1962. London: William Heinemann, 1963.
Reviews: (a) Fuson, B. W., *L. Jour.*, LXXXVII (Aug., 1962), 2754; (b) Guzzardi, W., *SRL*, XLV (Sept. 1, 1962), 30; (c) *Time*, LXXX (Sept. 14, 1962), 108.

16. *Boswell: The Ominous Years, 1774-1776*, ed. Charles Ryskamp and F. A. Pottle. New York: McGraw-Hill, 1963.
Reviews: (a) Abbott, C. C., *Listener*, LXX (1963-64), 28; (b) Adams, P., *Atlantic Mo.*, CCXI (June, 1963), 135; (c) Altick, R. D., *NYHTBR*, May 5, 1963, p. 6; (d) Balliett, W., *New Yorker*, XXXIX (June 29, 1963), 78; (e) *Critic*, XXI (April, 1963), 81; (f) Fuson, B. W., *L. Jour.*, LXXXVIII (Feb. 15, 1963), 771; (g) Halsband, R., *NYTBR*, April 21, 1963, p. 6; (h) Houpt, C. T., *Christian Science Monitor*, April 17, 1963, p. 9; (i) Pearson, H., *SRL*, XLVI (April 13, 1963), 26; (j) Seymour, W. K., *Contemporary Rev.*, CCIV (1963), 273-276; (k) *TLS*, Aug. 16, 1963, p. 626; (l) Wills, G., *Nat. Rev.*, XIV (July, 1963), 537.

17. *Boswell's Notebook, 1776-1777*, ed. A. Edward Newton. Buffalo: Privately Printed for R. B. Adam, 1919. A facsimile edition, limited to 50 copies.

18. *Boswell's Notebook, 1776-1777, Recording Particulars of Johnson's Early Life Communicated by Him and Others in Those Years*, ed. R. W. Chapman. London: Humphrey Milford, 1925. Printed from material in the R. B. Adam collection, with corresponding passages from the first edition of the *Life of Johnson* on opposite pages.
Reviews: (a) Depuis, A., *Revue Anglo-Americaine*, III (1925), 156; (b) Havens, R. D., *MLN*, XL (1925), 518.

EDITIONS

B. ESSAYS AND CORRESPONDENCE

19.   *Critical Strictures on the New Tragedy of Elvira, Written by Mr. David Malloch,* by James Boswell, Andrew Erskine, and George Dempster. London: W. Flexney, 1763.
Reviews: (a) *Critical Rev.,* XV (Feb., 1763), 160; (b) *Monthly Rev.,* XXVIII (Jan., 1763), 68.

19.1.   *Critical Strictures on the New Tragedy of Elvira Written by Mr. David Mallock, 1763. By James Boswell, Andrew Erskine, and George Dempster,* with an introduction by F. A. Pottle. Los Angeles: William A. Clark Memorial Library at the University of California, 1952. Augustan Reprint Society No. 35.

20.   *Dorando, A Spanish Tale,* by James Boswell. Glasgow: A. Foulis, 1767.
Reviews: (a) *Critical Rev.,* XXIV (July, 1767), 80; (b) *Gentleman's Mag.,* XXXVII (July, 1767), 361-362; (c) *Monthly Rev.,* XXXVII (July, 1767), 72; (d) *Scots Mag.,* XXIX (Appendix, 1767), 697.

20.1.   *Dorando, A Spanish Tale, by James Boswell.* London: Elkin Mathews and Marrot, Ltd., 1930.

21.   *The Hypochondriack; Being the 70 Essays by the Celebrated Biographer, James Boswell, Appearing in the London Magazine from November, 1777, to August, 1783, and Here First Reprinted,* ed. Margery Bailey. 2 vols. Palo Alto, California: Stanford University Press, 1928.
Reviews: (a) Chapman, R. W., *MLN,* XLIV (1929), 109-113; (b) Crane, R. C., *MP,* XXVI (1929), 375-376; (c) Pottle, F. A., *SRL,* V (Sept. 1, 1928), 88; (d) Redman, B. R., *Books,* July 15, 1928, p. 10; (e) *Revue de Litterature Comparée,* VIII (1928), 741; (f) *TLS,* Sept. 6, 1928, p. 629; (g) Windle, B. C., *Catholic World,* CXXVIII (March, 1929), 648-653.

22.   *Boswell's Column; Being His Seventy Contributions to the London Magazine under the Pseudonym The Hypochondriack from 1777 to 1783, Here First Printed in Book Form in England,* ed. with an introduction by Margery Bailey. London: W. Kimber, 1951.

23.   *Letters Between the Honourable Andrew Erskine and James Boswell, Esq.* London: S. Chandler for W. Flexney, 1763.
        Reviews: (a) *Critical Rev.,* XV (May, 1763), 343-345; (b) *London Chronicle,* XIII (April 28, 1763), 404-405; (c) *Monthly Rev.,* XXVIII (June, 1763), 476-479.

24.   *Boswell's Correspondence with the Honourable Andrew Erskine, and His Journal of a Tour to Corsica,* ed. George Birkbeck Hill. London: T. de la Rue and Co., 1879. Reprinted from original editions.

25.   *Letters of James Boswell, Addressed to the Reverend W. J. Temple. Now First Published from the Original MSS. With an Introduction and Notes,* ed. Sir Phillip Francis. London: Bentley, 1857.
        Reviews: (a) *Chambers's Journal,* XXVII (Feb. 7, 1857), 88-90; reprinted in *Eclectic Mag.,* XL (April, 1857), 548-551; (b) *The London Quarterly and Holborn Review,* VIII (July, 1857), 501-516.

26.   —————, with an Introduction by Thomas Seccombe. London: Sidgwick and Jackson, 1908.

27.   —————, ed. C. B. Tinker. 2 vols. Oxford University Press, 1924.
        Reviews: (a) Bacon, L., *SRL,* I (Feb. 28, 1925), 553-554; (b) Birrill, A., *New Statesman,* XXIV (Jan. 3, 1925), 364; (c) *Booklist,* XXI (April, 1925), 273; (d) Griffith, R. H., *Yale Rev.,* XV

(Oct., 1925), 170-172; (e) Hutchison, P. A., *NYTBR*, Jan. 25, 1925, p. 10; (f) *Independent*, CXIV (Feb. 7, 1925), 162; (g) MacDonald, W., *American Rev.*, III (May 25, 1925), 361; (h) Sherman, S. P., *NYHTBR*, Jan. 25, 1925, p. 1; (i) *Spectator*, CXXXIV, (Feb. 14, 1925), 244; (j) *TLS*, Jan. 15, 1925, p. 29; (k) Van Doren, M., *Nation*, CXX (March 25, 1925), 329; (l) Williams, S. T., *NAR*, CCXXII (Sept. 25, 1925), 189.

28.   *"On the Profession of a Player;" Three Essays by James Boswell, Now First Reprinted from the London Magazine for August, September, and October, 1770.* London: Elkin Mathews and Marrot, Ltd., 1929.
Review: *TLS*, Dec. 5, 1929, p. 1038.
Also see J. E. Agate (comp.). *English Dramatic Critics; An Anthology, 1660-1932*, pp. 51-54. New York: Hill and Wang, 1954, for excerpts.

28.1.   *The Correspondence of James Boswell and John Johnston of Grange.* The Yale Editions of the Private Papers of James Boswell. Research Edition: Correspondence Vol. I, ed. Ralph S. Walker. New York: McGraw-Hill, 1966.
Reviews: (a) Bottorff, W. K., *L. Jour.*, XCI (Aug., 1966), 3727; (b) Cruttwell, P., *Hudson Rev.*, XIX (1966), 638-688; (c) Hodgart, M., *New Statesman*, LXXII (Sept. 29, 1966), 447; (d) *TLS*, Jan. 12, 1967, p. 25; (e) Wills, G., *Nat. Rev.*, XVIII (Aug. 9, 1966), 790.

28.2   *The Correspondence and Other Papers of James Boswell Relating to the Making of the Life of Johnson.* The Yale Editions of the Private Papers of James Boswell. Research Edition: Correspondence Volume II, ed. Marshall Waingrow. New York: McGraw-Hill, 1970.

C. LIFE OF SAMUEL JOHNSON

29.   *The Life of Samuel Johnson, LL. D.*, by James Boswell, Esq. London: Henry Baldwin for Charles Dilly, in the Poultry, 1791.
Reviews: (a) *Critical Rev.*, II (New Series; July, 1791), 333-340; III (Nov.. 1791), 254-268; IV (March, 1792), 257-268; (b) *Edinburgh Mag.*, XIII (June, 1791), 501-505; (c) *English Rev.*, XVIII (July, 1791), 1-8; (Aug., 1791), 137-140; (d) *European Mag.*, XX (Aug., 1791), 107-110; (Sept., 1791), 189-193; (Nov., 1791), 371-374; (e) *Gentleman's Mag.*, LXI (May, 1791), 466-467; (June, 1791), 561-562; (Sept., 1791), 847-849; (Supplement, 1791), 1221; LXII (Jan., 1792), 49-50; (f) *Monthly Rev.*, VII (New Series; Jan., 1792), 1-9; (Feb., 1792), 189-198; VIII (May, 1792), 71-82; (g) *Scots Mag.*, LIV (Jan., 1792), 17-20.

30.   _____. Boston: Greenough and Stebbins for W. Andrews and L. Blake, 1807. First American Edition.

31.   _____, *Including a Journal of a Tour to the Hebrides, by James Boswell, Esq.*, ed. John Wilson Croker. 5 vols. London: John Murray, 1831.
Review: *Gentleman's Mag.*, CI (Aug., 1831), 141-144. See also Macaulay's extensive criticism, item 399 (Sept., 1831), 237-239.

32.   _____, ed. George Birkbeck Hill. 6 vols. Oxford University Press, 1887; Reprinted with different pagination in New York: Harper and Brothers, 1889.
Reviews: (a) Anderson, M. B., *Dial*, VIII (1887), 177; (b) *Athenaeum*, LXXXIX (June 25, 1887), 825-826; (c) Lounsberry, T. R., *Nation*, XLV (1887), 296; (d) Morgan, A., *Church Rev.*, L

(1887), 513; (e) Summers, W., *Congregational Rev.*, I (1887), 1023.

33.   *The Life of Samuel Johnson, LL. D., Together with Boswell's Journal of a Tour to the Hebrides and Johnson's Diary of a Journey Into North Wales,* ed. George Birkbeck Hill; rev. L. F. Powell. 6 vols. Oxford University Press, vols. I-IV, 1934; vols. V-VI, 1950 A considerably revised edition of vols. V and VI, by Powell, appeared in 1964. Reviews: (a) Bennett, C. H., *JEGP*, XXXIV (April, 1935), 256-259; (b) Kilbourne, R., *MLN*, LI (Dec., 1936), 552-554; (c) Sherburn, G., *PQ*, XIV (1935), 374-375; (d) Sutherland, J. R., *RES*, XII (Jan., 1936), 78-80; (e) *TLS*, June 28, 1934, pp. 449-450; (f) Tinker, C. B., *SRL*, XI (Jan. 26, 1935), 446-447; (g) Williams, H., *MLR*, XXX (July, 1935), 375-377.

34.   *The Life of Samuel Johnson, LL. D., by James Boswell, Esq.,* ed. Clement Shorter. New York: Gabriel Wells for Doubleday Page, 1922. The Temple Bar Edition. Individual introductions preface each of the ten volumes: A. L. Reade, Augustine Birrill, W. P. Trent, G. K. Chesterton, A. E. Newton, John Drinkwater, R. B. Adam, Walter de la Mare, C. B. Tinker, and R. A. King.

D. BIBLIOGRAPHY

35.   POTTLE, Frederick A. *The Literary Career of James Boswell, Esq., Being the Bibliographical Materials for a Life of Boswell.* Oxford University Press, 1929. Reprinted 1967. The only thorough primary Bibliography of Boswell's works. Reviews: (a) Crane, R. S., *Yale Rev.*, XIX (1930) 616-619; (b) *New Statesman*, XXXIII (June 8, 1929), 278; (c) Powell, L. F., *MP*, XXX (Aug.,

1932), 116-118; (d) Salpeter, H., *New York World Book Review*, Nov. 24, 1929, p. 10m; (e) *Spectator*, CXLIII (July 27, 1929), 129; (f) Stuart, D. M., *Nation and Athenaum*, XLV (June 15, 1929), 374; (g) T., G. M., *SRL*, VI (Aug. 10, 1929), 44; (h) Thompson, E. N. S., *PQ*, IX (Jan., 1930), 87-88.

35.1.   BROWN, Anthony E. "Boswellian Studies: A Bibliography," *Cairo Studies in English*, 1963-1966, pp. 1-75. Note: Other bibliographical materials may be found in items 213 and 600.1, Pottle's *CBEL* article, 1971 ed., the annual *PQ* bibliographies, and others in the field.

E. TRANSLATIONS (Arranged by languages)

36.1.   DANISH
a. *James Boswell. Dr. Johnson*, trans. Johanne Kastor Hansen. Copenhagen: Martin, 1942.
b. *Boswell I Holland (1763-1764)*, trans. J. Kastor Hansen. Copenhagen: Martin, 1952.
c. *London Dagbog, 1762-1763*, trans. J. Kastor Hansen. Copenhagen: Martin, 1951.

36.2.   FINNISH
Lontoon Päiväkirja 1762-1763, trans. Jouko Linturi. Helsinki: Tammi, 1952.

36.3   FRENCH
a. *Amours à Londres 1762-1763*, trans. Mme. E. R. Blanchet, with a preface by Andre Maurois. Paris: Hachette, 1952.
Reviews: (a) Doran, G., *Monde Nouveau Paru*, VIII (1952), 113-114; (b) Maurois, A., *Revue de Paris*, LIX (June, 1952), 3-9.
b. *Boswell Chez les Princes, 1765-1766*, trans. Celia Bertin, with a preface by Andre Maurois. Paris: R. Julliard, 1955.

    c. *Boswell Veut se Marier, 1766-1769*, trans. René Villoteau. Paris: Hachette, 1959.

    d. *Vie de Samuel Johnson*, trans. J. P. le Hoc. Paris: Galliard, 1954.

36.4.   **GERMAN**

    a. *Boswell's Grosse Reise, Deutschland und die Schweiz, 1764*, trans. Fritz Güttinger. Zurich: Diana Verlag, 1954; Stuttgart: Konstanz, Diana Verlag, 1955.

    b. *Dr. Samuel Johnson: Leben und Meinungen; Tagebuch einer Reise nach den Hebriden*, trans. Fritz Güttinger. Zurich: Manesse Verlag, 1951. An abridged edition.

    c. *Londoner Tagebuch, 1762-1763*, trans. Fritz Güttinger. Stuttgart and Zurich: Diana Verlag, 1953.

    d. *Tagebuch Einer Reise nach Den Hebridischen Inseln mit Doctor Samuel Johnson. Nach der Zweyten Ausgabe aus dem Englischen übersetzt*, trans. Albrecht Wittenberg. Lubeck: Bey Christian Gottfried Donatius, 1787.

36.5.   **ITALIAN**

    a. *Diario Londinese (1762-1763)*, trans. Augostino Lombardo. Torino: Einaudi, 1954.

    b. *Relazione della Corsica di Giacomo Boswell Scudiere Trasportata in Italiano dall Originale Inglese.* Stampato in Glatua nel 1768. Londra: Presso Williams. (Probably printed on the Continent.)

    c. *Samuel Johnson; Esperienza e Vita Morale, Conversazioni con Boswell.* Traduzione e Introduzione di Ada Prospero. Bari: G. Laterza e figli, 1939.

    d. *Vita di Samuel Johnson*, trans. Ada Prospero. vols. Milano: Garzanti, 1954. Apparently, the only complete translation to date.

36.6   **NORWEGIAN**

    Samuel Johnson's Liv, trans. Solveig Tunold. Oslo: Aschehoug, 1951.

36.7.   SWEDISH
a. *Dagbok I London 1762-1763*, trans. Anders Byttner. Stockholm: Natur och Cultur, 1951.
b. *Samuel Johnson's Liv*, trans. Harald Heyman. 4 vols., 1708-1778 only. Stockholm: Albert Bonniers Forlag, 1927.
Review of Vol. I: Pottle, F. A., *SRL*, III (May 14, 1927), 826.

36.8.   YUGOSLAV (Serbo-Croat)
Život Doktora Samuela Johnsona, trans. Stjepan Krešić. Zagreb: Naprijed, 1958.

SECTION TWO
Biographies of Boswell

37.   FITZGERALD, Percy H. *Life of James Boswell of Au-
        chinleck, with an Account of His Sayings, Do-
        ings, and Writings.* London: Chatto and Windus,
        1891; New York: D. Appleton and Co., 1891.
        Review: *Sat. Rev. Lit.* (London), LXXII (1891),
        507.

38.   LEASK, William Keith. *James Boswell.* Famous Scots
        Series. Edinburgh: O. Anderson and Ferrier,
        1896; New York: Charles Scribner's Sons, 1897.

39.   LEWIS, D. B. Wyndham. *The Hooded Hawk, or the
        Case of Mr. Boswell.* London: Eyre and Spottis-
        woode, 1946; New York: Longmans, Green Co.,
        1947. Reprinted as *James Boswell: A Short Life.*
        London: Eyre and Spottiswoode, 1952.
        Reviews: (a) Askwith, H., *SRL*, XXXI (Jan. 17,
        1948), 25; (b) *Christian Century*, LXIV (Dec. 17,
        1947), 1554; (c) Fremantle, A., *Commonweal*,
        XLVII (Jan., 1948), 375-377; (d) Henderson, R.
        W., *L. Jour.*, LXXII (Sept. 1, 1947), 1191; (e)
        Kirkus, XV (Aug. 1, 1947), 422; (f) *New Yorker*,
        XXIII (Nov. 22, 1947), 136; (g) Quennell, P.,
        New Statesman and Nation, XXXII (Dec. 21,
        1946), 465; (h) *TLS*, Jan. 4, 1947, p. 6; (i) Torre,
        L. de la, *NYTBR*, Dec. 14, 1947, p. 1; (j) Vul-
        liamy, C. E., *Spectator*, CLXXVIII (Jan. 3, 1947),
        17.

40.   TINKER, C. B. *Young Boswell. Chapters on James Bos-
        well, the Biographer, Based Largely on New Ma-
        terial.* London: G. P. Putnam's Sons, 1922; Bos-
        ton: The Atlantic Monthly Press, 1922. Covers
        especially the years 1740-1774.
        Reviews: (a) *Booklist*, XVIII (June, 1922), 328;

(b) *Dial*, LXXII (June, 1922), 650; (c) F., J., *Bookman*, LV (May, 1922), 299; (d) More, P. W., *Independent*, CVIII (July 8, 1922), 593; (e) Mulder, A., *Outlook*, CXXXII (Sept. 13, 1922), 78-80; (f) Murphy, E., *NYHTBR*, Sept. 3, 1922, p. 6; (g) Murry, J. M., *Nation and Athenaeum*, XXXII (Oct. 7, 1922), 18; (h) *New Republic*, XXX (May 24, 1922), 378; (i) *New Statesman*, XX (Oct. 14, 1922), 50; (j) *NYTBR*, April 9, 1922, p. 9; (k) *Pittsburgh Monthly Bulletin*, XXVII (July, 1922), 365; (l) *Spectator*, CXXIX (Oct. 14, 1922), 500; (m) *TLS*, Sept. 21, 1922, p. 21; (n) *Wisconsin Library Bulletin*, XVIII (June, 1922), 156.

41. VULLIAMY, Golwyn Edward. *James Boswell*. London: Geoffrey Bles, 1932; New York: C. Scribner's Sons, 1932.
     Reviews: (a) Fleming, P., *Spectator*, CXLIX (Dec. 2, 1932), 796; (b) Josephson, M., *New Republic*, LXXVI (Aug. 30, 1933), 80; (c) Kingsmill, H., *English Rev.*, LVI (March, 1933), 340-343; (d) Krutch, J. W., *Nation*, CXXXVI (April 5, 1933), 377; (e) Miles, H., *New Statesman and Nation*, IV (Dec. 10, 1932), 760; (f) *SRL*, IX (May 20, 1933), 607; (g) *Wisconsin Library Bulletin*, XXIX (June, 1933), 160.

41.1. POTTLE, Frederick Albert. *James Boswell: The Earlier Years, 1740-1769*. New York: McGraw-Hill, 1966.
     Reviews: (a) Carroll, J., *UTQ*, XXXVI (1967), 189-203; (b) *Choice*, III (Oct., 1966), 650; (c) Cruttwell, P., *Hudson Rev.*, XIX (1966), 683-688; (d) Daiches, D., *NYTBR*, June 19, 1966, p. 4; (e) Donovan, R. K., *L. Jour.*, XCI (July, 1966), 3404; (f) *Economist*, CCXXI (Nov. 12, 1966), 697; (g) Edel, L., *SRL*, XLIX (April 30, 1966), 30; (h) Furbank, P. N., *Listener*, LXXVI (1966), 325; (i) Hodgart, M., *New Statesman*, LXXII (Sept. 23, 1966), 447; (j) Kronenberger, L., *Book*

Week, May 22, 1966, p. 1; (k) Littlejohn, D., *Reporter*, XXXV (Nov. 3, 1966), 47; (l) Lonsdale, R., *Yale Rev.*, LVI (Oct., 1966), 117; (m) *Newsweek*, LXVII (May 23, 1966), 118; (n) Ross, I., *Studies in Scottish Literature*, V (1967), 60-67; (o) Sawyer, R., *Christian Science Monitor*, July 18, 1966, p. 9; (p) *Time*, LXXXVIII (July 1, 1966) 80; (q) *TLS*, Jan. 12, 1967, p. 25; (r) Wain, J., *New York Review of Books*, VI (June 9, 1966), 3; (s) Wills, G., *Nat. Rev.*, XVIII (Aug. 9, 1966), 790.

Note: A number of character sketches (See Index) and other minor biographical accounts of Boswell are listed under "General Studies." Perhaps the Mallory book (Item 409) and the Rogers *Memoir* are the most useful of the briefer biographical accounts. Some of the earlier sketches are very good, especially that of "H." (Item 311.1).

SECTION THREE
The Boswell Papers

Section Three
The Boswell Papers

42.   ABBOTT, Claude C. "Boswell's Mail-Bag," *London Times*, Nov. 21, 1936.

43.   _____. *A Catalogue of Papers Relating to Boswell, Johnson, and Sir William Forbes, found at Fettercairn House, A Residence of the Right Honourable Lord Clinton, 1930-1931.* Oxford University Press, 1936.
Reviews: (a) Greene, R. L., *MLN*, LIII (May, 1938), 384-387; (b) *TLS*, Jan. 16, 1937, p. 38; (c) Williams, H., *RES*, XIV (April, 1938), 230-231.

44.   _____. "The Heritage of Culture," *TLS*, March 5, 1949, p. 153. Abbott laments his being left out of much of the Boswell work.

45.   "All in?" *Time*, LVI (Oct. 2, 1950), 60. The most recent Boswell discoveries.

46.   ALTICK, Richard D. "The Secret of the Ebony Cabinet," *The Scholar Adventurers*, pp. 16-36. New York: Macmillan, 1950; *Bouillabaise for Bibliophiles, A Treasury of Bookish Lore*, pp. 101-125, ed. William Targ. New York: World Publishing Co., 1955. A thorough account of all the Boswell discoveries to date.

47.   BARKER, Felix. "Why Did We Sell This 'Great Literary Find' for £2,250?" *The Evening News* (London), Dec. 4, 1950. Quotes Abbott's complaints: see item 44.

48.   BASSO, Hamilton. "Boswell Detective Story," *Life*,

XXIX (Dec. 4, 1950), 93-94. An illustrated history of the discovery of the papers. Condensed in *Reader's Digest*, LVIII (March, 1951), 107-111.

49.   BIRRILL, Augustine. "Boswell Disrobed," *Et Cetera: A Collection, Etc.*, pp. 13-49. London: Chatto and Windus, 1930. Lists discoveries of *MSS* and gives editions of the *Life of Johnson*.

50.   "Boola Boswell," *Time*, LIV (Aug. 8, 1949), 42. The Isham collection arrives at Yale.

51.   "Boswell Discovery," *Scholastic*, LIII (Nov. 17, 1948), 12.

52.   "Boswell's Ebony Cabinet," *Living Age*, CCCXXXIII (Nov. 1, 1927), 837-838. Isham's discovery.

53.   "Boswell the Incomparable," *Outlook*, CXLVII (Oct. 5, 1927), 141. Isham's collection.

54.   "Boswell-Johnson Papers," *Pub. Weekly*, CLIV (Nov. 20, 1948), 2148. First exhibition of Isham's collection.

55.   "Boswell's *Journal of Hebrides* made Thirty-three per cent Longer," *Literary Digest*, CXXII (Nov. 7, 1936), 29-30. A brief history of Isham's discoveries.

56.   "Boswell Papers," *JRLB*, XXII (Oct., 1938), 314-316. Legal history of Isham's Boswell MSS.

57.   "The Boswell Papers," *TLS*, Sept. 22, 1927, p. 652.

58.   _____, *TLS*, Aug. 12, 1949, p. 528. Further discussion of the Yale collection.

59.   "Boswell Transfer is Second in a Year," *New York Times*, Aug. 1, 1949.

60. "Boswell's Troubles," *Newsweek*, XXXVI (Nov. 6, 1950), 96-97. Abbott's find at Fettercairn House.

61. BRONSON, Bertrand H. "Boswell's Boswell," *Johnson Agonistes and Other Essays*, pp. 53-99. Cambridge University Press, 1946. How Boswell reveals himself in his work. See also item 161.

62. BRYSON, John N. "Boswell's Executors," *TLS*, Oct. 6, 1927, p. 694.

63. CHAPMAN, R. W. "Boswell's Archives," *Essays and Studies by Members of the English Association*, XVII (1932), 33-43. Boswell's will and his relatives.

64. "The Compleat Boswell," *Time*, LII (Nov. 29, 1948), 102, 104. Isham and the Boswell *MSS*.

65. EISENMAN, Alvin. "Designing and Manufacturing the Boswell Papers," *Pub. Weekly*, CLVIII (Sept. 2, 1950), 967-970. Techniques of the McGraw-Hill editions.

66. ESDAILE, Arundel. "Boswell Redivivus," *QR*, CCXCI (Jan., 1953), 94-104.

67. _____. "Sir W. Forbes' Boswell Papers Found," *LAR*, XXXVIII (April, 1936), 164.

68. FIFER, C. N. "Editing Boswell: A Search for Letters," *Manuscripts*, VI (1935), 2-5.

69. HASLAM, W. H. "Geoffrey Scott and Colonel Isham," *TLS*, July 15, 1955, p. 397. Scott's work with the Malahide papers.

70. HOPKINS, F. M. "Rudge to Publish Boswell Papers," *Pub. Weekly*, LXII (Dec. 3, 1927), 2050-2052.

71. HYDE, Mary C. "History of the Johnson Papers,"
    Bibliographical Society of America Papers, II
    (1951) 103-116.

72. ISHAM, Col. Ralph H. "Geoffrey Scott," *SRL*, VI
    (Aug. 24, 1929), 74. A remembrance of and a tri-
    bute to Geoffrey Scott.

73. LESLIE, Shane. "The Boswell Papers," *The Saturday
    Review* (London), CXLIX (March 29, 1930), 381-
    382; (April 5, 1930), 414-415. Boswell's lite-
    rary friends in England and on the Continent.

74. —————. "Boswelliana," *The Saturday Review*
    (London), CLXX (July 18, 1931), 79-81; (July 25,
    1931), 111-113. The latest published volumes of
    Isham's limited edition (item 1), Vols. X-XII.

75. LIEBERT, Herman W. "The Boswell Papers," *Yale
    Alumni News*, Oct., 1949, pp. 14-16.

76. "Malahide Papers," *Time*, XXVII (March 9, 1936),
    79. Isham's methods of acquiring the Boswell
    papers.

77. "The Malahide and Fettercairn Papers," *TLS*, Dec.
    18, 1948, p. 270. *MSS* discoveries to date.

78. MORLEY, Edith J. "Boswell in the Light of Recent Dis-
    coveries," *QR*, CCLXXII (Jan., 1939), 77-93. An
    appraisal of the work at Yale to date.

79. "New Boswell Papers Bought by Yale Library," *Pub.
    Weekly*, CLVIII (Sept. 30, 1950), 1587. 100 pa-
    ges of the *Life of Johnson* MS found at Mala-
    hide.

80. "Original Boswell Papers," *SRL*, IV (Oct. 1, 1927),
    163. Isham's purchases arrive in America.

81. POTTLE, F. A. "The Yale Editions of the Private Papers of James Boswell," *Ventures*, II (Winter, 1963), 11-15.

82. _____, and Marion S. Pottle. *Catalogue of an Exhibition of the Private Papers of James Boswell from Malahide Castle*. New York: Grolier Club, 1930.

83. _____. *The Private Papers of James Boswell from Malahide Castle...: A Catalogue*. London: Oxford University Press, 1931.

84. "The Private Papers of James Boswell," *Pub. Weekly*, CXV (Jan. 5, 1929), 43-45.

85. "Promise and Achievement," *TLS*, Aug. 7, 1948, p. 442.

86. "A Publishing Enterprise Completed," *Pub. Weekly*, CXXV (March 17, 1934), 1150-1151. Comment on the final two volumes of item 1.

87. ROBERTS, S. C. "Boswell Revealed," *Spectator*, CLXXXI (Dec. 3, 1948), 727. Publication of the papers.

88. TINKER, C. B. "Boswell Letters," *TLS*, July 29, 1920, p. 488. The query that, perhaps, brought the reply, "Try Malahide Castle."

89. WHITRIDGE, Arnold. "More Boswell," *SRL*, VII (Nov. 22, 1930), 361-362. Discusses item 1.

90. "Whittlesey House to Publish Boswell Collection," *Pub. Weekly*, CLVI (Aug. 6, 1949), 576-578. Plans for publication of the papers.

91. "Yale Acquires New Group of Boswell Papers," *New York Times*, Sept. 21, 1950.

92.   "Yale Acquires New Group of Boswell Works," *New York Herald Tribune*, Sept. 21, 1950.

93.   "Yale Appoints Committee to Advise on Boswell Papers," *Pub. Weekly*, CLVI (Dec. 3, 1949), 2280-2281.

SECTION FOUR
General Studies

Section Four
General Studies

93.1.   A. [Hugo Arnot (?)]. "Of Out-doors Proceedings in the Douglas Cause," *Scots Mag.*, XXIX (Appendix, 1767), 696-698. A discussion of *Dorando*, item 20.

93.2.   A., E. E. "A Conjecture on the Early Writings of Dr. Johnson," *Gentleman's Mag.*, LXIV (May, 1794), 426. Comments on the *Life of Johnson*.

94.   ABBOTT, Claude C. *Boswell: The Robert Spence Watson Memorial Lecture for 1945-1946.* Newcastle-Upon-Tyne: Literary and Philosophical Society, 1946.

95.   _____. "New Light on Johnson and Boswell," *Listener*, XLI (May 19, 1949), 853-854. A history of the Boswell journals.

95.1.   ACADEMICUS. *Gentleman's Mag.*, LXIII (March, 1793), 236. Comments on the *Life of Johnson*.

96.   ADAMS, J. Donald. "Speaking of Books: A Discussion of James Boswell's Book," *NYTBR*, June 23, 1946, p. 2. Praises Geoffrey Scott's work.

97.   ADAMS, Sarah F. "Boswell's *Life of Samuel Johnson*," *YULG*, XXIX (1954), 35-36. Cancels in vol. II, 1791 edition.

98.   ALGAR, F. "Boswell's 'Life of Johnson,'" *NQ*, CLXXXII (Aug. 29, 1942), 141-142. Answers Powell's query no. 16; see item 510.

98.1.   ALKON, Paul K. "Boswell's Control of Aesthetic Distance," *UTQ*, XXXVIII (1969), 174-191.

98.2.   AMORY, H. "Boswell in Search of the Intentional Fallacy," *BNYPL*, LXXIII (Jan., 1969), 24-39.

98.3.   ANDERSON, G. P. "Pascal Paoli: An Inspiration to the Sons of Liberty," *Publications of the Colonial Society of Massachusetts*, XXVI (1924-1926), 188. Boswell's *Corsica* in America.

98.4.   ANDERSON, Patrick. *Over the Alps: Reflections on Travel and Travel Writing with Special Reference to the Grand Tours of Boswell, Beckford, and Byron* London: Hart-Davis, 1969.

99.   ANDREWS, H. C. "Boswell's 'Life of Johnson,'" *NQ*, CLXXXII (1942), 235. Answers Powell's query no. 8; see item 510.

99.1.   *Anecdotes of the Learned Pig, with Notes Critical and Explanatory and Illustrations from Bozzy, Piozzi, Etc.* London, 1786.

99.2.   "Ann Seward," *Gentleman's Mag.*, LXXXI (Aug., 1811), 154-156; (Sept., 1811), 241-246; (Oct., 1811), 350-353. A *Life of Johnson* comment.

99.3.   "Anna Seward," *Gentleman's Mag.*, LXIV (Feb., 1794), 120-121. A comment on the *Life of Johnson*.

99.4.   ANTI-STILETTO. "Vindication of Dr. Johnson and Mr. Boswell," *Gentleman's Mag.*, LVI (Jan., 1786), 17-23. A defense of Boswell's *Hebrides*.

100.   ASHMUN, Margaret. *The Singing Swan: An Account of Anna Seward and Her Acquaintance with Dr. Johnson, Boswell, and Others of Their Time.* With a preface by F. A. Pottle. New Haven: Yale University Press; London: Oxford University Press, 1931.

GENERAL STUDIES

101.   ATTALUS [William Mudford]. "Dialogues of the Dead. Boz and Poz in the Shades," *A Critical Inquiry into the Moral Writings of Dr. Samuel Johnson.... Containing a Dialogue between Boswell and Johnson in the Shades*, pp. 129-144. London: C. Corrall for Messrs. Cobbett and Morgan, and R. Faulder, 1802, 1803. First published in *The Porcupine*, London, Oct. 3-Dec. 26, 1801.

101.1   B. "Character of Mr. Boswell," *Gentleman's Mag.*, LXV (June, 1795), 471-472. A sketch.

101.2   B. "Johnson," *Gentleman's Mag.*, LXIV (Jan., 1794), 18. An omission in the *Life of Johnson*.

101.3.   B., J. "The Conversation Between Dr. Johnson and Mrs. Knowles," *Gentleman's Mag.*, LXVI (Nov., 1796), 924. In the *Life of Johnson*.

101.4.   B., J. "Memoirs and Character of Edmond Malone," *Gentleman's Mag.*, LXXXIII (June, 1813), 513-520. See especially pp. 518-520 for an account of Boswell's relationship with Malone.

102.   B., N. "Boswell," *NQ*, IV (Ser. 2; July 11, 1857), 29. Caricatures of Boswell's *Hebrides*. See item 177; the caricatures are listed in item 548.

103.   BACON, L. "'Evening in Great Portland Street': James Boswell Speaks to His Son Alexander; A Poem," *Literary Rev.*, IV (March 15, 1924), 593.

103.1.   BAILEY, J. C. *Dr. Johnson and His Circle*. London: Williams and Nergate; New York: Henry Holt and Co., 1913. Revised and edited by L. F. Powell London: Oxford University Press, 1944. See especially chapters 2 and 3.

104.   BAILEY, John (ed.). *Johnson and Boswell in the High-*

lands. Abridged from Johnson's "Journey to the Western Islands" and Boswell's "Journal of a Tour to the Hebrides." London and Edinburgh: T. Nelson and Sons, 1926.

105. BAILEY, Margery. "Boswell as Essayist," *JEGP*, XXII (1923), 412-423. Boswell's *Hypochondriack* papers. See item 166.

106. ――――――. "James Boswell: Lawyer or Press Agent?" *Dalhousie Rev.*, X (Jan., 1931), 481-494.

107. BALDWIN, Louis. "The Conversation in Boswell's *Life of Johnson*," *JEGP*, LI (1952), 492-506. Boswell's accuracy in recording Johnson's words.

108. BARFIELD, O. "Boswell," *New Statesman*, XVII (Aug. 13, 1921), 520.

109. BARKER, F. W. E. "Boswell's Record of Johnson's Table-Talk," *Papers of the Manchester Literary Club*, XLIII (1917), 93-114.

110. BATTY, W. R. "Boswell's Shorthand," *TLS*, Aug. 4, 1932, p. 557. Reply to item 489.

111. BAUMANN, A. A. "The Tardy Bust," *Living Age*, CCLIX (Oct. 31, 1908), 309-312. Boswell's statue in Lichfield. See item 141.

112. BEALS, Frank L. *Boswell in Chicago.* Chicago: Privately Printed, 1946. Records of the Chicago Boswell Club.

113. BEAULAVON, Georges. "Les Derniers Moments d' Apres Les Papiers Intimes de Boswell," *Revue Métaphysique et de Morale*, XIV (1939), 471-476

GENERAL STUDIES

114.   BELLOC, Hilaire. "Boswell," *Silence of the Sea, and Other Essays*, pp. 71-75. London: Sheed and Ward, Inc., 1940.

115.   BENNETT, Charles H. "The Auchinleck Entail," *TLS*, Feb. 27, 1937, p. 151. Boswell's inheritance.

116.   ————. "A Boswell Reference," *TLS*, May 18, 1940, p. 248. Beaumont and Fletcher in the *Life of Johnson*.

117.   BENNETT, James O. "Boswell's 'Life of Samuel Johnson,'" *Much Loved Books: Best Sellers of the Ages*, pp. 197-203. New York: Liveright Publishing Corp., 1927.

117.1. BENVOLIO. "The Battledoor Kept up for Boswell's Shuttlecock," *Gentleman's Mag.*, LVI (Feb., 1786), 122-126. Defends Boswell's *Hebrides*.

117.2. ————. "Johnson's Biographers," *Gentleman's Mag.*, LVI (April, 1786), 302-304.

118.   BERGENGREN, R. "Boswell's Chapbooks and Others," *Lamp*, XXVIII (Feb., 1904), 39-44.

119.   BERNARD, F. V. "Two Errors in Boswell's *Life of Johnson*," *NQ*, CCIV (July-Aug., 1959), 280-281. Johnson's use of parentheses and "the former and the latter" constructions.

120.   BETTANY, W. A. Lewis. *Johnson's Table Talk. A Selection of His Main Topics and Opinions Taken from Boswell's Life....* London: Blackie and Son, 1904.

121.   ————. "The Making of Boswell's 'Johnson,'" *TLS*, Feb. 13, 1930, p. 122. Correspondence be-

tween Temple and Forbes and Malone. See item 302 and item 408.

122. BIANCOLLI, Louis L. (ed.). *Book of Great Conversations*, pp. 67-80; 106-136. New York: Simon and Schuster, 1948.

123. BICKNELL, P. F. "Prince of Interviewers," *Dial*, XXXVIII (March 1, 1905), 141-144.

124. BIOGRAPHICUS [A Scottish Lady]. "Letter," *Gentleman's Mag.*, LXV (Aug., 1795), 634. On Boswell's character.

125. BIRRELL, Augustine. "Boswell as Biographer," *In the Name of the Bodleian*, pp. 133-139. New York: Charles Scribner's Sons, 1905; *Collected Essays and Addresses, 1880-1920*, I, 150-154. 3 vols. London: J. M. Dent, 1922. Attacks Carlyle's essay, item 184.

126. _____. "Corsica Boswell," *Living Age*, CCCXVIII (Sept. 29, 1923), 609-612. Boswell and Paoli in Corsica.

127. _____. "Johnson's 'Journey' and Boswell's 'Journal,'" *Nation and Athenaeum*, XXXV (Aug. 9, 1924), 591-592.

127.1 "Bishop of Derry and Mr. Boswell," *Gentleman's Mag.*, LV (Sept., 1785), 741-742. Concerns Boswell's *Letter to the People of Scotland*, 1785.

128. BLUNDEN, Edmund C. "Boswellian Error," *Votive Tablets; Studies Chiefly Appreciative of English Authors and Books*, pp. 160-166. New York: Harper and Bros., 1932.

129. BOLTON, John H. *A Commentary and Questionnaire*

on *Selections from Boswell's Life of Johnson.* London: Sir I. Pitman and Sons, 1928.

129.1. BOND, W. H., and Daniel E. Whitten. "Boswell's Court of Session Papers: A Preliminary Checklist," *Eighteenth Century Studies in Honor of Donald F. Hyde,* ed. W. H. Bond, pp. 231-255. New York: Grolier Club, 1970.

130. BOOTH, Wayne C. "The Morley Boswell," *Chicago Rev.,* VII (Winter, 1953), 36-46. A fictional spoof.

131. BOSTOCK, John K. *A. E. Klausing's Translation of Boswell's "Corsica" with Four Facsimiles.* Oxford University Press, 1931. Privately Printed.

132. BOSWELL, Sir Alexander, Bart. *A Letter to James Boswell from His Son Alexander, A Schoolboy, Relative to the Life of Samuel Johnson, then in Progress.* Princeton University Press, 1948. 101 limited copies.

133. "Boswell and Boswelliana," *Edinburgh Rev.,* CV (Jan., 1857), 456-493. Comments on items 25, 31, and 423.

134. "Boswell—Early Life of Johnson," *QR,* CIII (April, 1858), 279-328. Comments on items 25, 31, and 423.

135. "Boswell and the Girl from Botany Bay," *TLS,* May 7, 1938, p. 322. See item 478.

136. "Boswell and Goldsmith," *Outlook,* XCVII (March 18, 1911), 580-581. Boswell's treatment of Goldsmith.

137. "Boswell and His Editors," *Church QR,* XXVII (Oct.,

1888), 121-138. Gives history of editions of the *Life* and *Hebrides*, especially in the 1880's.

138.   "Boswell and His Ego: Some Bi-Centenary Reflections; A Reputation Redressed," *TLS*, Oct. 26, 1940, pp. 542, 545. A biographical sketch.

139.   "Boswell and His Father," *Blackwood's Mag.*, CCXXIII (March, 1928), 325-342.

139.1.   BOSWELL, James. "Defence of Johnson's Veracity," *Gentleman's Mag.*, LXIII (Nov., 1793), 1008-1011. Boswell's controversy with Anna Seward. See under Seward in the Index for other items.

139.2.   _____. "Mr. Boswell and the Gastrells," *Gentleman's Mag.*, LXII (Jan., 1792), 18. See item 453.1.

139.3.   _____. "Reply to Miss Seward's second Attack," *Gentleman's Mag.*, LXIV (Jan., 1794), 32-34. The Seward controversy.

139.4.   _____. "To Dr. Smollett," *Monthly Mag.*, XIX (June 1, 1805), 464-465. Boswell's letter to Smollett concerning Corsica.

139.5.   _____. "Two Letters by Boswell," *Gentleman's Mag.*, LVI (April, 1786), 285-286. Boswell defends *Hebrides*.

140.   BOSWELL, James, Jr. *Bibliotheca Boswelliana. A Catalogue of the Entire Library of the Late James Boswell.* London: J. Compton, 1825.

141.   "Boswell in Lichfield," *Outlook*, XC (Nov. 7, 1908), 515-516. Boswell's statue in the town square. See item 111.

GENERAL STUDIES

142.   "Boswell Memorial in London," *Outlook*, CIX (March 24, 1915), 670-671. Preservation of Boswell's homes. See items 377 and 623.

143.   BOSWELL, R. Bruce. "Letter of James Boswell," *NQ*, IX (Ser. 8; May 16, 1896), 384. A letter, dated Edinburgh, 11 April, 1774, in the possession of this author, published for the first time.

144.   "Boswell's Epitaph," *Gentleman's Mag.*, LXV (June, 1795), 525. The shield on Boswell's coffin.

145.   "Boswell and Shakespeare Problems," *TLS*, May 16, 1929, p. 408. The "Conjugal Fidelity" deletion. See item 218.

146.   "Boswell's 'Johnson,'" *Temple Bar*, XCV (June, 1892), 251-258. Calls Boswell a faultless biographer.

147.   "Boswell's Letters," *Irish Metropolitan Mag.*, I (1857), 576-597. Comments on item 25.

148.   "Boswell's Letters to Temple," *Living Age*, LII (Feb., 1857), 631-637. Comments on item 25.

148.1.   "Boswell's Life," *Gentleman's Mag.*, LXIII (Nov., 1793), 1030-1032; LXIX (Jan., 1794), 60-63. Discusses the second edition of the *Life of Johnson*.

148.2.   —————, *The Monthly Mirror*, VIII (Sept., 1799), 154. Comments on the third edition of the *Life of Johnson*.

149.   BOTTRALL, Margaret. *Every Man a Phoenix: Studies in 17th Century Autobiography*. London: John Murray, 1958.

150.   ———— (ed.). *Personal Records*, pp. 157-160, 216. London: Rupert Hart-Davis, 1961.

151.   Bouchier, Jonathan. "Boswell," *NQ*, IX (Ser. 4; Feb. 3, 1872), 102. Gray's 1768 letter to Walpole. See items 154 and 622.

152.   ————. "Boswell versus Lockhart," *NQ*, II (Ser. 9; Sept. 10, 1898), 206. Compares them as biographers.

153.   ————, *NQ*, II (Ser. 9; Oct. 15, 1898), 306-307. In praise of Lockhart.

154.   ————. "Gray and Boswell," *NQ*, VIII (Ser. 4; Nov. 25, 1871), 433. Gray's 1768 letter to Walpole. See items 151 and 622.

155.   Boys, Richard. "Boswell on Spelling," *MLN*, LIII (1938), 600. Defends Boswell's orthography in the *Corsica* Journal, item 7.

156.   ————. "Sir Joshua Reynolds and the Architect Vanbrugh: A Footnote to Boswell," *Papers of the Michigan Academy of Science, Arts, and Letters*, XXXIII (1947), 323-336.

157.   "Bozzies," *Eliza Cook's Jour.*, XXVI (Feb., 1853). Reprinted in *Eclectic Mag.*, XXIX (July, 1853), 382-385. English biography and Boswell.

158.   Bracy, Robert. "Corsica Boswell," *Eighteenth Century Studies*, 28-36. Oxford: Blackwell, 1925.

159.   Bradley, Rose M. "Boswell and a Corsican Patriot," *Nineteenth Century*, LXVII (Jan., 1910), 130-145. Boswell and Paoli's campaign.

159.1. Brady, Frank. *Boswell's Political Career*. New Haven: Yale University Press, 1965. See item 656.

159.2. BRINITZER, Carl. *Dr. Johnson und Boswell. Begeg-nung und Freundschaft.* Mainz: Florian Kupfer-berg Verlag, 1968. Rev.: Belanger, Terry. *New Rambler,* VI (Ser. C: Jan., 1969), 52-53.

159.3. BRISTOLENSIS. *Gentleman's Mag.,* LVI (Sept., 1786), 735-737. Omissions in *Hebrides.*

160. BRITT, Albert. "Johnson and Boswell," *The Great Biographers,* pp. 67-76. New York: Whittlesey House, 1936.

161. BRONSON, Bertrand H. "Boswell's Boswell," *Johnson and Boswell: Three Essays. University of Calif-ornia Publications in English,* Vol. III, no. 9, pp. 363-475. Berkeley and Los Angeles: Univer-sity of California Press, 1944.

162. ―――――. "Samuel Johnson and James Boswell," *Major British Writers,* II, 1-17, ed. George B. Harrison. 2 vols. New York: Harcourt, Brace and Co., 1954.

163. BROOKS, A. R. "The Literary and Intellectual Foun-dations," *Dynamic America,* XIV (1942), 752-753.

163.1. ―――――. "The Scottish Education of James Bos-well," *Studies in Scottish Literature,* III (1966), 151-157.

164. ―――――. "Pleasure and Spiritual Turmoil in Bos-well," *CLAJ,* III (1959), 12-19.

165. BROWN, J. T. T. "James Boswell: An Episode of His Grand Tour (1763-1766)," *Transactions of the*

Glasgow Archaeological Society, New Series, VII (1920), 197-215.

166.   _____. "James Boswell as Essayist," *Scotch Historical Rev.,* XVIII (1921), 102-116.

167.   . "The Youth and Early Manhood of James Boswell," *Proceedings of the Royal Philosophical Society of Glasgow,* XLI (1909-1911), 219-245.

167.1.   BROWN, Terence. "America and Americans as Seen in James Boswell's *The Life of Samuel Johnson, LL. D.,*" *New Rambler,* VI (Ser. C; Jan., 1969), 44-51.

168.   BROWNING, David C. (comp.). "James Boswell," *Everyman's Dictionary of Literary Biography,* pp. 66-67. London: J. M. Dent and Sons; New York: E. P. Dutton and Co., 1958. Revised edition, 1960.

169.   BRYANT, D. C. "Edmund Burke and His Friends," *Washingtion University Studies in Language and Literature,* IX (1939), 99-135.

170.   BUCKLEY, W. E. "Boswell's 'Life of Johnson,'" *NQ,* VII (Ser. 7; June 29, 1889), 513. Points out errors in pagination in vol. 2, 1791 edition.

170.1.   BUTT, John. *Biography in the Hands of Walton, Johnson, and Boswell.* Ewing Lectures. Los Angeles: University of California Press, 1966.

171.   _____. *James Boswell.* University of Edinburgh Inaugural Lecture, No. 3, Friday 11th December 1959. Edinburgh: Oliver and Boyd, Ltd., 1959.

172.   BUTTERFIELD, L. H. *Benjamin Rush's Reminiscences*

of Boswell and Johnson. Princeton University Press, Privately Printed for the Donald F. Hydes, 1946.

173. Buxton, Charles R. "Boswell's 'Life of Johnson,'" *A Politician Plays Truant: Essays on English Literature*, pp. 83-99. London: Christophers, 1929.

173.1. Byblius. *Gentleman's Mag.*, LV (Dec., 1785), 942-943. Excesses in *Hebrides*.

174. C. "Boswellian Personages," *NQ*, III (Ser. 2; May 2, 1857), 354. Last living persons who appear in the *Life of Johnson.* See item 376.

174.1. C. "James Boswell," *Gentleman's Mag.*, LXV (June, 1795), 469-471.

175. C., F. "Boswell's Johnson," *NQ*, VIII (Ser. 1; Nov. 5, 1853), 439. Correction of a Johnson quote from Horace in the *Life.* See item 283.

176. C., J. "Obituary," *Gentleman's Mag.*, LXV (June, 1795), 469-471. Boswell's last views on religion.

177. C., W. "Boswell Caricatures," *NQ*, V (Ser. 2; March 27, 1858), 265. Reply to item 102, and see item 548.

178. C., W. H. "Macaulay on Boswell," *NQ*, IV (Ser. 8; Aug. 19, 1893), 158. Reply to item 433, and see item 399.

179. C's., R. "Bacon a Poet," *NQ*, IV (Ser. 1; Dec. 13, 1851), 474. A reference in *Hebrides.* See items 439 and 473.

180. Caldwell, Joshua W. "A Brief for Boswell," *Sewanee*

Rev., XIII (July, 1905), 336-351. A defense of Boswell's character against his critics.

181. CANBY, Henry S. "Boswell's Johnson," *Definitions, Essays in Contemporary Criticism*, pp. 249-253. New York: Harcourt, Brace and Co., 1922-1924. Second Series.

182. _____. "What Professor Tinker Cut," *New Repub.*, XLII (March 25, 1925), 127. See items 308 and 589.

183. CAREW-HUNT, R. N. "A Fragment of Boswelliana," *Nineteenth Century and After*, CXLII (1947), 243-248. Correspondence between Boswell's children and Mr. Heaviside, a surgeon.

184. CARLYLE, Thomas. "Boswell's Life of Johnson," *Critical and Miscellaneous Essays*, III, 49-104. 7 vols. London: Chapman and Hall, 1888. Reprinted from *Fraser's Mag.*, V (May, 1832), 379-413. See Item 125.

185. CARNIE, R. H. "Boswell's Projected History of Ayrshire," *NQ*, CC (June, 1955), 250-251. An Outline found in the *Boswell Papers*, vol. 12, p. 53.

186. _____. "A Letter from Lord Hailes to James Boswell in Holland," *NQ*, CXCIX (Feb., 1954), 63-65. Prints Dalrymple's letter of 27 June, 1764.

187. CARVER, George. "Boswell and the 'Johnson,'" *Alms for Oblivion: Books, Men, and Biography*. (Science and Culture Series), pp. 160-169. Milwaukee: Bruce Publications, 1946. The making of the *Life of Johnson*.

188. CHALMERS, Alexander. *A Lesson in Biography, or*

How to Write the Life of One's Friend. Being an Extract from the Life of Dr. Pozz witeen by James Bozz, Esq., 1798. Edinburgh: Privately Printed by the Aungervyle Society Reprints, 4th series, 1887. A Parody.

189. CHAMBERS, Robert. *A Dictionary of Eminent Scotsmen.* 5 vols. with supplements. Glasgow: Blackie, 1855.

190. _____. "James Boswell," *Chamber's Cyclopedia of English Literature,* II (1780-1876), 336. 2 vols. London and Edinburgh: W. and R. Chambers, 1876.

191. CHANCELLOR, E. Beresford. "The Age of Johnson," *The Literary Ghosts of London,* pp. 202-212. London: Richards, 1933. Boswell and Johnson, with special reference to their homes and friends in London.

192. CHAPMAN, R. W. "Birkbeck Hill's Johnson," *TLS,* July 26, 1923, p. 504. Plans for re-editing.

193. _____. "Boswell's Editors," *TLS,* Sept. 14, 1946, p. 439. An entry in the *Life* misplaced by editors.

194. _____. "Boswell's Proof-Sheets," *London Mercury,* XV (1925), 50-58, 171-180.

195. _____. "Boswell's Revises of the *Life of Johnson,*" *Johnson and Boswell Revised by Tehemselves and Others,* pp. 21-50. Oxford University Press, 1928.

196. _____. "Cancels in Boswell's 'Hebrides,'" *Bodleian Quarterly Record,* IV (July, 1924), 124.

197. ————. "Dr. Johnson in Scotland," *The Portrait of a Scholar*, pp. 127-140. Oxford University Press, 1922.

198. ————. "The Hill-Powell Boswell," *TLS*, Dec. 31, 1938, p. 827. A progress report.

199. ————. "Hill's Boswell," *SRL*, XI (March 23, 1935), 564. Reply to Tinker's review, item 33(f).

200. ————. "Johnson and Boswell," *TLS*, March 2, 1946, p. 103. Dates Summer, 1784, correspondence.

201. ————. "The Johnson-Boswell Correspondence," *NQ*, CLXXXV (July 17, 1943), 32-39. A chronological record of the correspondence. See item 202.

202. ————, *NQ*, CLXXXVI (1944), 45-47. Corrects item 201.

203. ————. *Johnson, Boswell, and Mrs. Piozzi: A Suppressed Passage Restored*. Oxford University Press, 1929. Concerns *Hebrides* journal.

204. ————. *Johnsonian and Other Essays and Reviews*. Oxford University Press, 1953. Reprints various essays and reviews by Chapman on Johnson, Boswell, and others.

205. ————. "Johnson's Letter to Boswell," *RES*, XVIII (1942), 323-328.

206. ————. "Johnson's Letters: Notes on Boswell's Text," *TLS*, Feb. 25, 1939, p. 128; March 4, 1939, p. 140. Boswell's excellence in the *Life of Johnson*.

GENERAL STUDIES

206.1.   —————(ed.). *The Letters of Samuel Johnson.* 3 vols. Oxford University Press, 1952.

207.   —————. *Two Centuries of Johnsonian Scholarship.* Glasgow: Jackson, Son and Co., 1945. Murray Lecture, 1945. The importance of Boswell.

208.   —————, L. F. Powell, and D. Nichol Smith. *Johnson and Boswell Revised by Themselves and Others.* Three essays. Oxford University Press, 1928. See separate titles, by authors, items 195 and 513.

209.   "Character of Dr. Johnson: From Mr. Boswell's Tour," *Gentleman's Mag.*, LV (Oct., 1785), 756-757. Descriptions of Johnson in *Hebrides.*

209.1.   CHARNWOOD, Dorothea Roby (Thorpe), Lady. "A Habitation's Memories," *Cornhill Mag.*, LXIII (Nov.-Dec., 1927), 535-547.

210.   CHESTERTON, G. K. "Boswell's 'Johnson,'" *Good Words*, XLIV (Nov., 1903), 774-777.

211.   CHITTELDROOG. "Public Teachers," *NQ*, IX (Ser.4; Jan. 13, 1872), 42-43. Croker and Carlyle; See items 598 and 599.

211.1.   CLARKE, Maragret. "Boswell: Scot. Nat.," *New Saltire*, No. 10, Dec., 1963, pp. 28-30. A letter to the Bishop of Derry.

212.   CLIFFORD, James L. (ed.). *Biography as an Art; Selected Criticism 1560-1960*, pp. 50-53 *et passim.* Oxford University Press, 1962. Quotations from and random comments on Boswell. Bibliography.

212.1.   —————. *From Puzzles to Portraits: Problems of a Literary Biographer.* Chapel Hill: University of

North Carolina Press, 1970. Passim references to Boswell's *Life*.

212.2. ―――――. *Twentieth Century Interpretations of Boswell's Life of Johnson*. Englewood Cliffs, New Jersey: Prentice Hall, 1970. Includes select bibliography.

213. ―――――. *Johnsonian Studies: A Survey and Bibliography*. Minneapolis: University of Minnesota Press, 1951. Revised and expanded as *Samuel Johnson: A Survey and Bibliography of Critical Studies*. Minneapolis: University of Minnesota Press, 1970. See item 600.2.

213.1. COLE, Richard C. "James Boswell and the Irish Press, 1767-1795," *BNYPL*, XXIII (Nov., 1969), 581-598.

213.2. ―――――. "The Sitwells and James Boswell: A Genealogical Study," *Genealogists Mag.*, XV (1967), 402-406.

214. COLEMAN, William H. "The Johnsonian Conversational Formula," *QR*, CCLXXXII (1944), 432-445. Boswell's comments on Johnson's conversation.

215. COLLINS, Joseph. *The Doctor Looks at Biography*, p. 25ff. New York: Doubleday Doran, 1925.

216. COLLINS, P. A. W. "Boswell's Contact with Johnson," *NQ*, CCI (April, 1956), 163-166. Days on which Boswell may have met with Johnson.

217. ―――――. *James Boswell*. London: Longmans for the British Council and the National Book League, 1956. A brief history.

218. "Conjugal Fidelity: A Suppressed Dialogue between

Boswell and Johnson," *Life and Letters*, IV (1930), 164-166. Concerns the 'double standard.' See item 145.

219. "Conversations with Rousseau," *SRL*, XXXVI (Oct. 3, 1953), 15-16. A preview, with excerpts, of item 5.

220. COPELAND, Thomas W. "Boswell's Portrait of Burke," *The Age of Johnson: Essays Presented to C. B. Tinker*, pp. 27-39. New Haven: Yale University Press, 1949. Also in Copeland's *Our Eminent Friend, Edmund Burke*. New Haven: Yale University Press, 1949. A vivid description of Burke in the *Life of Johnson*.

220.1. _____. "Unpublished Burke Papers," *TLS*, Sept. 30, 1949, p. 640.

220.2. CORE, G. "Boswellian Aether," *Sewanee Rev.*, LXXVI (1968), 686-690.

221. CORNEY, Bolton. "Boswell and His Editors," *NQ*, XII (Ser. 1; Oct. 27, 1855), 328. Lists editions of the *Life* through Croker (1831). Reply to item 442.

222. _____. "Johnson versus Boswell," *NQ*, X (Ser. 1; Dec. 9, 1854), 471. Boswell's arithmetic in the *Life*. Reply to item 236 and see also items 237 and 530.

222.1. "Corrections and Additions to the First Edition of Mr. Boswell's Life of Dr. Johnson," *The British Critic*, III (Jan.-June, 1793), 191-192. Comments on the second edition of the *Life*.

223. CORRIGAN, Beatrice. "Guerrazzi, Boswell, and Corsica," *Italica*, XXXV (1958), 25-37.

224. COSULICH, G. "Johnson's Affection for Boswell," *Sewanee Rev.*, XXII (April, 1914), 151-155.

225. COWIE, Alexander. "A Boswell Misquotation," *TLS*, April 25, 1936, p. 356.

226. Cox, James E. "The Independent Boswell and the Capricious Dr. Johnson," *Quarterly Journal of the University of North Dakota*, XXII (Fall, 1931), 51-59.

227. "Critical Comment on 'An Epistle to James Boswell, etc.," *Gentleman's Mag.*, LX (May, 1790), 436. See item 258.

228. CROKER, J. Wilson, and John Wilson. "Nocte's Ambrosianae," *Blackwood's Mag.*, XXX (Nov., 1831), 802-846. Revised and printed as *Answers to Mr. Macaulay's Criticism in the Edinburgh Review on Mr. Croker's Edition of Boswell's Life of Johnson*. London: John Murray, 1856. See item 399.

229. CROSS, Wilbur L. *An Outline of Biography from Plutarch to Strachey*, pp. 29-32. New York: Henry Holt and Co., 1924. Compares Boswell with Sterne in ability to portray character. Reprinted from *Yale Rev.*, XI (Oct., 1921), 140-157.

230. CROSSLEY, James. "Boswell and the Hackman Hanging," *NQ*, IV (Ser. 3; Sept. 19, 1863), 232-233. Boswell and a murderer. See item 553.

231. D., A. H. "Boswell's 'Matrimonial Thought,'" *NQ*, II (Ser. 6; July 30, 1880), 8. Asks the identity of "M. H." to whom the poem is addressed. See item 485.

GENERAL STUDIES

231.1.   D., W. &. *Gentleman's Mag.*, LXIV (April, 1894), 328-329. Johnson's views on religion.

232.   DAICHES, David. *A Critical History of English Literature*, II, 794-796. 2 vols. New York: The Ronald Press, 1960. Discusses Boswell's Journals as autobiography.

233.   DANKERT, Clyde E. "Adam Smith and James Boswell," *QQR*, LXVIII (1961), 323-332. Discusses them as contemporary Scotsmen.

234.   D'ARBLAY, Madmae (Fanny Burney). "James Boswell," *Portraits in Prose*, pp. 209-210, ed. Hugh McDonald. New Haven: Yale University Press, 1947.

234.1.   DAVIES, Eileen C. "An Epigram on Boswell," *NQ*, CCXII (1967), 182.

234.2.   DAY, Douglas. "Boswell, Corsica, and Paoli," *English Studies*, XLV (Feb., 1964), 1-20.

234.3.   DEBEER, E. S. "Macaulay and Croker: The Review of Croker's Boswell," *RES*, X (New Ser.; 1959), 388-397.

235.   DECASTRO, J. Paul. "Laetitia Hawkins and Boswell," *NQ*, CLXXXV (1943), 373-374. Notes from Miss Hawkins' diary concerning Boswell and Francis Barber.

235.1.   DEELMAN, Christian. *The Great Shakespeare Jubilee.* New York: Viking Press, 1964. See Deelman's index for references to Boswell.

236.   DEMORGAN, A. "Boswell's Arithmetic," *NQ*, X (Ser. l; Nov. 4, 1854), 363-364. Points out an error no editor of the *Life* has yet corrected. See items 222, 237, and 530.

237. _____, *NQ*, XI (Ser. 1; Jan. 27, 1855), 57. See items 222, 236, and 530.

238. DENVIR, Bernard. "Guillaume Martin," *TLS*, Nov. 4, 1955, p. 657. Identity of a person appearing in item 6, p. 7.

239. DILWORTH, E. N. "Boswell in America," *NQ*, CCIII (May, 1958), 220. Passages from Boswell's Corsica in a 1769 Boston almanac.

240. DIXON, J. "Boswell's 'Tour to the Hebrides': A Misquotation," *NQ*, XII (Ser. 6; Nov. 14, 1885), 386-387. Boswell's paraphrase of Virgil.

240.1. "Dr. Johnson," *Gentleman's Mag.*, LXIV (Nov., 1794), 1001. Comments on the second edition of the *Life*.

241. "Dr. Johnson Dines Out," *Golden Book*, XX (Aug., 1934), 179.

242. "The Doctor, via Bozzy, to the Laird," *Month at Goodspeed's Bookshop*, IX (March, 1938), 195-199. Johnson's *Journey to the Western Isles* taken to Lord Raasay by Boswell.

243. DOBSON, Austin. "Boswell's Predecessors and Editors," *A Paladin of Philanthropy*, pp. 137-172. London: Chatto and Windus, 1899. Same as item 245.

244. _____. *Dr. Johnson's Haunts and Habitations*. *Introduction to Boswell*, ed. A. Glover. N. p., 1901. Reprinted by Sidewalk Series, 1902.

245. _____. *Miscellanies*, pp. 109-143. New York: Dodd, Mead and Co., 1898. Same as item 243.

246. DRINKWATER, John. "Johnson and Boswell," *The Muse in Council*, pp. 218-224. London: Sidgwick and Jackson, 1925. Johnson without Boswell.

247. "Dubious Character of Johnson," *Gentleman's Mag.*, LV (Dec., 1785), 942-943. Compares Johnson and Swift.

248. DUESBERG, Jacques. "Boswell, l'Incorrigible," *Synthèsés*, VIII (March, 1956), 408-410.

249. DUKE, Winifred. "Boswell Among the Lawyers," *Juridical Rev.*, XXXVIII (1926), 341-370. Boswell's study and practice of the law.

250 DUNN, Charles E. "James Boswell and His Book," *Advance*, CXXXIII (1941), 5-6.

251. DUNN, Waldo H. *English Biography*, pp. 112-129; 157-160, *et passim*. London: J. M. Dent and Sons, Ltd.; New York: E. P. Dutton and Co., 1916. Influences of the *Life* on later biographical practice.

252. _____. "Jamie Boswell's Thorn in the Flesh," *SAQ*, XXVIII (Jan., 1929), 71-82. Boswell and Peter Pindar.

253. DUSCHNES, Philip and Fanny. *The Last Boswell Paper*. Woodstock, Vermont: Elm Tree Press, 1951. A reprint of Krutch's spoof, item 374.

253.1. E. "Miscellaneous Remarks," *Gentleman's Mag.*, LXIV (Aug., 1794), 728. Comments on the *Life*.

254. E., B. E. "Boswell, Soame Jenyns, Lyttelton, and

Smollett," *NQ*, XII (Ser. 2; July 20, 1861), 48. Asks for connection of Boswell and these men.

254.1.   EBORACENSIS. *Gentleman's Mag.*, LXIV (June, 1794), 508-510. Harsh criticism of the *Life*.

255.   EDEL, Leon. *Literary Biography: The Alexander Lectures, 1955-1956*, pp. 13-20. London: Rupert Hart-Davis; University of Toronto Press, 1957. Boswell helped Johnson live his life.

256.   ELOVSON, Harold. '"Mr. Kristrom' in Boswell's 'Life of Johnson,'" *MLR*, XXVII (1932), 210-212. Identity of Kristrom suggested.

257.   ELTON, Oliver. "Boswell," *A Survey of English Literature, 1730-1780*, I, 153-159. 2 vols. New York: Macmillan, 1928. Boswell's career.

258.   *Epistle to James Boswell, Esq., Occasioned by His Long-Expected and Now Speedily-to-be-Published, Life of Dr. Johnson.* London: Printed for J. Hookham, Bond Street, 1790. See items 227 and 597.

259.   ESDAILE, Arundel. "Boswell in His Diaries," *Autolycus' Pack, and Other Light Wares; Being Essays, Addresses, and Verses*, pp. 74-92. London: Grafton and Co., 1940.

260.   _____. "Boswell in His Diaries," *LAR*, XXXVI (Feb., 1934), 34-40.

261.   _____. "A Footnote to Boswell," *TLS*, Oct. 23, 1937, p. 783. Boswell and Edward Dilly.

262.   _____, and Edmund Esdaile. "Boswell on the Grand Tour," *QR*, CCXCIV (Oct., 1956), 464-474. A brief account of Boswell's travels.

GENERAL STUDIES

262.1. "Extract of a Letter from Mr. Boswell," *Gentleman's Mag.*, XXXVII (April, 1767), 187. Concerns Corsica.

263. FADIMAN, Clifton. "Party of One," *Holiday*, XVI (Aug. 1954), 6-8.

263.1. FAULKNER, Will. "An Original Letter of Dr. Johnson," *Gentleman's Mag.*, LXIV (Feb., 1794), 100-101. A new letter not quoted in the *Life*. Page 100 is misprinted "January" in some copies.

264. FEUSS, Claude M. "The Biographer and His Victims," *Atlantic Mo.*, CXLIX (Jan., 1932), 62-73. Boswell mentioned as "the standard to which the pedagogically-minded still hearken."

265. _____. "Debunkery and Biography," *Atlantic Mo.*, CLI (March, 1933), 347-356.

266. FIFER, C. N. "Boswell and the Decorous Bishop," *JEGP*, LXI (Jan., 1962), 48-56. Boswell and Bishop Percy.

267. _____. "Boswell's Langton and the River Wey," *NQ*, CCI (Aug., 1956), 347-349. Treatment of Langton in the *Life*.

268. _____. "Dr. Johnson and Bennett Langton," *JEGP*, LIV (1955), 504-506. Boswell's "too brief" description of their meeting.

269. FILIOLUS. "Dr. Parr and Mr. Boswell," *Gentleman's Mag.*, LXV (May, 1795), 392-393. Reply to item 459; see also items 312 and 534.

270. FILON, Augustin. "Boswell's Love Story," *Fortnightly Rev.*, LXXXVI (New series LXXX) (1906), 487-495. Boswell and Zelide. See item 310.

271.   FITCH, George H. "Old Dr. Johnson and His Boswell," *Comfort Found in Good Old Books*, pp. 116-123. San Francisco: Paul Elder, 1911.

272.   FITZGERALD, Percy. "Boswell's Autobiography," *QR*, CCXIV (Jan., 1911), 24-44. Boswell reveals himself in the *Life*.

273.   _____. *Boswell's Autobiography*. London: Chatto and Windus, 1912.

274.   _____. *A Critical Examination of Dr. G. Birkbeck Hill's "Johnsonian" Editions*. London: Bliss, Sands and Co., 1898. See item 583.

275.   _____. *Croker's Boswell and Boswell. Studies in the "Life of Johnson."* London: Chapman and Hall, 1880.

276.   _____. *Editing à la Mode. An Examination of Dr. Birkbeck Hill's New Edition of Boswell's "Life of Johnson."* London: Ward and Downey, 1891.

276.1.   _____. *Further Examination of Dr. Birkbeck Hill's Edition of Boswell's Life of Johnson*. London, 1891.

276.2.   _____. *More Editing à la Mode: Being a Further Examination of Dr. Birkbeck Hill's Edition of Boswell's Life of Johnson*. London: Sweeting, 1892.

277.   _____. "Some Bozzyana," *Gentleman's Mag.*, CCXCII (Feb., 1902), 191-203. Boswell's library and his correspondence with John Wilkes.

278.   _____. "Some New Lights on 'Bozzy,'" *NCR*, IJ (1897), 209-218, 328-340.

279.   FITZHUGH, Harriet L., and P. K. Fitzhugh. *Concise Biographical Dictionary of Famous Men and Women*, pp. 68-69. Revised and enlarged. New York: Grosset, 1949.

280.   FITZ-PATRICK, W. J. "Boswell's Letters to the Rev. W. J. Temple," *NQ*, III (Ser. 2; May 16, 1857), 381-382. Suggests identity of "La Belle Irlandaise." See item 281.

281.   —————. "James Boswell," *NQ*, V (Ser. 8; Feb. 24, 1894), 145. Thirty-seven years later, another suggestion for the identity of "La Belle Irlandaise." See item 280.

282.   FLECTHER, Edward G. "Mrs. Piozzi on Boswell and Johnson's Tour," *University of Texas Studies in English*, XXXII (1953), 45-58.

283.   FORBES, C. "Boswell's Johnson," *NQ*, VIII (Ser. 1; Dec. 3, 1853), 551. A correction of Johnson's quotation from Horace. See item 175.

284.   FORTESCUE-BRICKDALE, Charles. "Dr. Johnson and Mrs. Macaulay: The Credibility of Boswell," *NQ*, CLIX (Aug. 16, 1930), 111-112. Calls Boswell in error in the story of Mrs. Macaulay's footman.

285.   FOSTER, Finley. "Piozzian Rhymes," *TLS*, March 30, 1933, p. 230. Boswell's attack on Piozzi's *Anecdotes*. See item 644.

286.   FRANK, Thomas. "Two Notes on Giuseppe Baretti in England: Baretti and Boswell...," *Annali Instituto Universitario Orientales, Napoli: Sezione Germanica*, II (1959), 239-263. See item 629.

287.   FREEMAN, Robert M. *The New Boswell*. London: John Lane, 1923. A parody of the *Life*.

288.   FUSSELL, Paul, Jr. "The Force of Memory in Boswell's
         London Journal," *SEL*, II (Summer, 1962), 351-
         357.

288.1.   ————. "Memorable Scenes of Mr. Boswell,"
         Encounter, XXVIII (May, 1967), 70-74.

288.2.   G. "A Johnsonian Contribution," *Gentleman's Mag.*,
         LXIV (Nov., 1794), 1001. An omission in the
         Life.

289.   G. "Scottish Legal Ballad," *NQ*, I (Ser. 4; Jan. 11,
         1868), 42. A question of authorship.

290.   GALLAWAY, W. F. "Boswell and Sterne," *Letters*, V
         (1931), 21-25; 30.

291.   GARDINER, Alfred G. "On Boswell and His Miracle,"
         Pebbles on the Shore, pp. 64-69. New York: E. P.
         Dutton and Co., 1917.

292.   GARLICHITHE. "Boswell and Malone's Notes on Mil-
         ton," *NQ*, X (Ser. 1; July 8, 1854), 29. Asks if
         the notes were published.

293.   GARNETT, Richard, and Edmund Gosse (eds.). "James
         Boswell," *English Literature: An Illustrated
         Record*. Vol. III: *Milton to Johnson*, Chap. IV:
         "The Age of Johnson," pp. 336-342. 4 vols. New
         York: Grosset and Dunlap, 1903.

294.   GARTON, Charles, "Boswell and Dr. Gordon," *Dur-
         ham University Journal*, XLVI (1954), 63-64.

295.   ————. "Boswell's Favourite Lines from Horace,"
         NQ, CCIII (Dec., 1958), 306-307. Passages from
         Horace's *Satires*, II, i.

GENERAL STUDIES

296.   GARRATY, John. *The Nature of Biography*, pp. 25-28; 93-99. New York: Alfred A. Knopf, 1957.

297.   GASELEE, Stephen. "Boswell to Reynolds, 1775," *NQ*, CLXXVI (June 17, 1939), 427. Reply to item 443.

297.1. "General State of Affairs Abroad and at Home," *Gentleman's Mag.*, XXXVIII (Dec., 1768), 585. Comments on Boswell's *Corsica*.

297.2. GIBBON, Edward, and Georges Deyverdun. *Memoires Litteraires de la Grande Bretagne, pour l'an 1768*. London: C. Heydinger, 1769. Contains a harsh comment on *Corsica*.

298.   GISSING, A. "Appleby School: An Extra-Illustration to Boswell," *Cornhill Mag.*, LX (April, 1926), 404-414.

299.   GLOVER, T. R. "Boswell," *Poets and Puritans*, pp. 175-210. London: Methuen and Co., 1916.

299.1. GODET, P. *Madame de Charriere et Ses Amis*. 2 vols. Geneva, 1906. An early account of Boswell and Zélide.

299.2. GOLDEN, James L. "Boswell on Rhetoric and Belles-Lettres," *Quarterly Journal of Speech*, L (1964), 266-276.

300.   GOLDIE, Noel B. "Boswell on the Northern Circuit," *Spectator*, CLXXXI (Dec. 10, 1948), 763; (Dec. 17, 1948), 808-809. A Boswell adventure.

301.   GORDON, George (Charles C. Baldwin). "Boswell's 'Life of Johnson,'" *More Companionable Books*, pp. 31-36. London: Chatto and Windus, 1947.

302.   GOULD, Rupert T. "The Making of Boswell's Johnson." *TLS*, Feb. 27, 1930, p. 166. See items 121 and 408.

303.   Gow, A. S. F. "The Unknown Johnson," *Life and Letters*, VII (Sept., 1931), 200-215.

303.1.   GRATIAN. *Gentleman's Mag.*, LVI (Feb., 1786), 122-124.

304.   GRAY, James. "Boswell's Brother Confessor: William Johnson Temple," *Tennessee Studies in Literature*, IV (1959), 61-71.

305.   GRAY, W. Forbes. "Dr. Johnson in Edinburgh," *QR*, CCLXIX (Oct., 1937), 281-297. Boswell's and Johnson's accounts of the Scotland tour.

306.   ————. "James Boswell in the Newer Light," *QR*, CCLXXXIII (Oct., 1945), 456-467. Reviews past two decades of Boswellian scholarship.

307.   ————. "New Light on James Boswell," *Juridical Rev.*, L (1938), 142-164. Boswell's family and friends.

308.   "The Greatest of All Biographers," *Current Opinion*, LXXVIII (April, 1925), 429-432. Comments on items 182 and 589.

309.   GREEN, M. [John Nichols] "Boswell and His Patron, Dodsley," *Gentleman's Mag.*, LXV (June, 1795), 471-472. Comments on Boswell's *Cub at New-Market*.

309.1.   GREENACRE, Phyllis. "The Family Romance of the Artist," *The Psychoanalytic Study of the Child*, XIII (1958), 9-43.

GENERAL STUDIES

309.2.   GREENE, Donald J. "Reflections on a Literary Anni-
         versary," *QQR*, LXX (1963), 198-208. The day
         Boswell and Johnson first met.

309.3.   GREENE, Edward Burnaby. "Corsica, an Ode," *Lon-
         don Chronicle*, Nov. 8, 1768, p. 445. Praises Bos-
         well. See item 450, VIII, 89.

310.   GRIBBLE, Francis. "Boswell's Dutch Flirtation," *The
         Nineteenth Century and After*, LXXII (Nov.,
         1912), 942-952. The life of Zélide after her af-
         fair with Boswell. See also item 270.

311.   GULICK, Sidney L., Jr. "Johnson, Chesterfield, and
         Boswell," *The Age of Johnson: Essays Presented
         to C. B. Tinker*, pp. 329-340. New Haven: Yale
         University Press, 1949. The *Life fo Johnson* be-
         fore 1763.

311.1.   H. "Memoir of James Boswell," *Monthly Mag.*, XV
         (July 1, 1803), 543-553. A biographical sketch.
         See item 442.1.

311.2.   H., D. "Dr. Johnson and Dr. Parr," *Gentleman's
         Mag.*, LXV (April, 1795), 284-285. Boswell's de-
         scription of their meeting.

312.   _____. "Strictures on Boswell," *Gentleman's
         Mag.*, LV (Dec., 1785), 959. See items 269, 459,
         and 534.

313.   H., O. N. "Boswell's 'Life of Johnson': Translations,"
         NQ, CLXXVII (Nov. 11, 1939), 351. Asks how
         many there are. See item 482 for reply.

314.   HADDEN, J. Cuthbert. "Johnson and Boswell in Scot-
         land," *Gentleman's Mag.*, CCXCVIII (June,
         1905), 597-605.

315.   HALL, Amanda B. "Johnson's Boswell; Through the Hebrides," *SRL*, XXVII (Nov. 11, 1944), 26.

316.   HAMILTON, Harlan W. "Boswell's Suppression of a Paragraph in *Rambler 60*," *MLN*, LXXVI (March, 1961), 218-220. An omission from the *Life*. See the Hill-Powell edition, I, 32-33.

317.   HAMM, Victor M. "Boswell's Interest in Catholicism," *Thought*, XXI (Dec., 1946), 649-666. Reviews Boswell's religious life.

318.   HARASTI, Zoltan. "The Life of Johnson," *More Books*, XIII (March, 1938), 98-112.

319.   HARRISON, Frederic. "Great Biographies," *Among My Books*, pp. 65-66. London: Macmillan, 1912.

320.   HART, Edward. "The Contributions of John Nichols to Boswell's Johnson," *PMLA*, LXVII (June, 1952), 391-410. Boswell's use of Nichols' *Anecdotes*.

321.   HART, F. R. "Boswell and the Romantics: A Chapter in the History of Biographical Theory," *ELH*, XXVII (1960), 44-65. The influence of Boswell in the early Nineteenth-century.

321.1.   HARTLEY, Lodovic. "A Late Augustan Circus: Macaulay on Johnson, Boswell, and Walpole," *SAQ*, LXVII (1968), 513-526.

322.   HAZEN, Allen T. "Boswell's Cancels in the 'Tour to the Hebrides,'" *Bibliographical NQ*, II (1938), 7.

323.   HEGEMAN, Daniel Van Brunt. "Boswell and the Abt Jerusalem, A Note on the Background of *Wer-*

ther," JEGP, XLIV (1945), 367-369. Boswell in Germany.

324. ⎯⎯⎯⎯⎯. "Boswell's Interviews with Gottsched and Gellert," *JEGP*, XLVI (1947), 260-263.

325. HENDERSON, James S. "James Boswell and His Practice at the Bar," *Juridical Rev.*, XVII (1905), 105-115. Boswell's legal career as it is found in the *Scottish Law Reports.*

326. HENLEY, W. E. "Boswell," *Views and Reviews: Essays in Appreciation*, pp. 194-200. London: David Nutt, 1892. Croker and Macauley.

326.1. HENN, J. "Original Anecdotes of Dr. Johnson," *Gentleman's Mag.*, LXIII (May, 1793), 408.

327. HETHERINGTON, John. *The Tour to the Hebrides: Its Value to the Social Historian.* Lichfield Johnson Society, 1948.

328. HILL, George Birkbeck. "Boswell's Proofsheets," *Atlantic Mo.*, LXXIV (Nov., 1894), 657-668. Hill's examination of the MSS in the R. B. Adam collection. Also in *Johnson Club Papers*, pp. 51-80. London: T. Fisher and Unwin, 1899.

329. ⎯⎯⎯⎯⎯. *The Boswell Centenary, May 19, 1895.* Privately Printed, 1895.

330. ⎯⎯⎯⎯⎯. "The Centenary of Boswell," *MacMillan's Mag.*, LXIV (May, 1891), 37-43. Reprinted in *Living Age*, CXC (July 4, 1891), 27-33. Boswell's character.

331. ⎯⎯⎯⎯⎯. *Dr. Johnson: His Friends and His Critics.* London: Smith Elder, 1878.

332.   ⸻. *Footsteps of Dr. Johnson.* London: Sampson Low, Marston and Co., 1890.

333.   HIRN, Yrjo. *Dr. Johnson och James Boswell.* Lund: Gleerup, 1922; Helsingfors: Holger Schildts Förlagsaktiebolag, 1922.

334.   HITSCHMAN, Edward. "Boswell: The Biographer's Character," *Psychoanalytic Quarterly*, XVII (1948), 212-225. Reprinted in *Great Men: Psychoanalytic Studies*, pp. 186-198. New York: International Universities Press, 1956.

335.   HOLCROFT, Thomas. *Memoirs.* 3 vols. London: Phillips, 1816.

336.   HOOVER, Andrew. "Boswell's Letters at Newhailes," *UTQ*, XXII (1953), 244-260. Correspondence with David Dalrymple, Lord Hailes. See item 337

337.   ⸻. "Boswell's First London Visit," *VQR*, XXIX (1953), 242-256. Unpublished letters. See item 336.

338.   HORNE, Colin J. "Boswell, Burke, and the 'Life of Johnson,'" *NQ*, CXCV (1950), 498-499. Boswell's *Life* outsold Burke's *French Revolution*.

339.   ⸻. "Boswell and Literary Property," *NQ*, CXCV (July 8, 1950), 296-298. Boswell's copyright of the *Life*. See item 643.

340.   ⸻. "Malone and Steevens," *NQ*, CXCV (Feb. 4. 1950), 56. Steevens's aid in compiling the *Life*.

341.   HOUSTON, Benjamin F. "James Boswell," *NQ*, CCVIII (April, 1963), 154. A letter to John Johnston in 1768. See item 28.1, p. 243.

GENERAL STUDIES

342. "How Many Issues Are There of the First Edition of Boswell's *Life of Johnson?*" *BNYPL*, XXXI (Oct., 1927), 826-827. Suggests there were 2 or 3.

343. HUNT, R. W. "The Malahide and Fettercairn Papers," *TLS*, Jan. 8, 1949, p. 25. A Boswell gift to the Bodleian Museum.

344. HUNTER, Richard A., and Ida Macalpine. "Alexander Boswell's Copies of *The Anatomy of Melancholy*, 1621 and 1624," *Book Collector*, VI (1957), 406-407.

345. HYDE, Mary C. "The History of the Johnson Papers," *Papers of the Bibliographical Society of America*, XLV (1951), 103-116.

345.1. I., I. D. "Remarks on the Various Biographers of Johnson," *Gentleman's Mag.*, LVI (Supplement, 1786), 1123-1127.

346. INGE, Charles C. "Two More Boswell Letters," *TLS*, March 27, 1930, p. 274. Letters to Ralph Churton.

347. IRVING, William H. *The Providence of Wit in the English Letter Writers*, pp. 300-306, *et passim*. Durham, N. C.: Duke University Press, 1955. Boswell as a correspondent.

348. ISHAM, Col Ralph H. (ed.). *Voltaire's Letter Written from the Chateau de Ferney, Feb. 11, 1765.* New York: William Rudge, 1927. Facsimile reproduction.

349. ————, J. W. Krutch, and Mark Van Doren. "James Boswell, *The Life of Samuel Johnson,*" *The New Invitation to Learning*, ed. Mark Van Doren, pp. 283-296. New York: Random House, 1942.

349.1.   Isles, Duncan E. "Other Letters in the Lennox Collection," *TLS*, Aug. 5, 1965, p. 685.

349.2.   Ives, Sidney. "Boswell Argues a Cause: Smith, Steel, and 'Actio Redhibitoria,'" *Eighteenth Century Studies in Honor of Donald F. Hyde*, ed. W. H. Bond, pp. 257-265. New York: Grolier Club, 1970.

349.3.   J., B. "To Edmond Malone," *Gentleman's Mag.*, LVI (Jan., 1786), 66-67. A poem addressed to Malone, perhaps by Boswell.

350.   J., G. "Illustration of 'Boswell's Johnson'," *NQ*, VIII (Ser. 2; Aug. 6, 1859), 107. A parallel passage in *Hebrides* and *King Lear*.

350.1.   Jaarsma, Richard J. "Boswell the Novelist: Structural Rhythm in the *London Journal*," *North Dakota Quarterly*, XXXIV (1966), 51-60.

350.2.   Jack, Ian. "Two Biographers: Lockhart and Boswell," *Johnson, Boswell, and Their Circle; Essays Presented to L. F. Powell in Honour of His Eighty-fourth Birthday*, pp. 268-285. Oxford University Press, 1965.

351.   "James Boswell," *Eclectic Mag.*, XLIV (May, 1858), 136-137. A brief biographical sketch.

352.   ————, *Nouvelle Biographie Générale*, Vol. 5, p. 832. Paris: Firmin Didot, Freres, Editeurs, 1855.

353.   "James Boswell; A Study," *Temple Bar*, LVI (1879), 314-332.

354.   James, W. [Walter James Head, later Sir Walter James, Bart.] *A Defence of Mr. Boswell's Journal; in a Letter to the Author of the Remarks*

signed *Verax*. London: W. T. Swift, 1785. See item 614.

354.1. JENNINGS, Louis J. (ed.). *The Croker Papers. The Correspondence and Diaries of the Late Right Honorable John Wilson Croker, LL. D., F. R. S., Secretary to the Admiralty from 1809 to 1830.* 3 vols London: John Murray, 1884. See especially II, 24-49.

355. "Johnson as a Christian and a Critic," *Eclectic Mag.*, XXXIV (April, 1855), 492-500. Reprinted from the *Eclectic Review*: IX (Feb., 1855), 152-168. Croker's edition of the *Life*.

356. JOHNSON, C. F. "James Boswell," *Columbia University Course in Literature, Based on the World's Best Literature*, Vol. 12. 18 vols. New York: Columbia University Press, 1928-1929.

357. JOHNSON, Edgar. "Eighteenth Century Apogee," *One Mighty Torrent: The Drama of Biography*, pp. 217-233. New York: Stackpole Sons, 1937; Macmillan Co., 1955. Boswell's ability to entertain. See index for other references.

358. _____. "Grand Cham," *A Treasury of Biography*, pp. 162-204. New York: Howell, Soskin Co., 1941.

359. *Johnsoniana; or, Supplement to Boswell*. London: John Murray, 1836.

359.1. "A Johnsonian Argument," *Gentleman's Mag.*, LXIII (Dec., 1793), Last page of Index, Unpaginated.

360. JOHNSON, Lionel P. "Bustling, Breathless, Bragging Boswell," *Academy*, LII (Sept. 18, 1897), 213-214. Comments on item 38.

361. —————. "Boswell," *Post Liminium: Essays and Critical Papers*, pp. 136-142, ed. Thomas Whittemore. New York: Mitchell Kennerly, 1912.

362. JOHNSONOPHILUS. "Johnsoniana, from Boswell's *Journey*, with Remarks," *Gentleman's Mag.*, LV (Dec., 1785), 967-969. Johnson's contradictions of Boswell's statements.

363. JOHNSTON, James C. *Biography: The Literature of Personality*. London and New York: Century Co., 1928. See index for references.

364. JONES, Evan (ed.). *The Father, Letter to Sons and Daughters*, pp. 50-52. New York: Rinehart, 1960.

365. JUVENIS, Miles. "Boswell in Normandy," *Spectator*, CLXXIII (Sept. 1, 1944), 193. A traveller takes a copy of Boswell's *Life* on a tour.

366. KANKI, S. "Boswell's Art as a Biographer," *Studies in English Literature* (Imperial University, Tokyo, Japan), XIII (1933), 154-160.

367. KEITH, Alexander. "Boswell's Boswell," *Listener*, XXIV (Nov. 7, 1940), 667-668.

368. KENRICK, W. *An Epistle to James Boswell, Esq., Occasioned by His Having Transmitted the Moral Writings of Dr. Samuel Johnson to Pascal Paoli.* .London: N. p., 1768.

369. KENT, M. "Lichfield Group," *Cornhill Mag.*, CLVIII (Sept., 1938), 347-352.

369.1. KERSLAKE, John. *Mr. Boswell*. London: Her Majesty's Stationery Office, 1967. A catalog of an exhibition in the National Portrait Gallery.

370. KEVIN, Neil. "Johnson Talking," *Irish Ecclesiastical Record*, LVIII (Ser. 5; Nov., 1941), 401-413.

370.1. KILEY, Frederick S. "Boswell's Literary Art in the *London Journal*," *CE*, XXIII (May, 1962), 629-632.

371. KIRWAN, H. N. "The Boswell Supplement," *London Mercury*, XXVII (1933), 331-340.

372. KRONENBERGER, Lewis. "Johnson and Boswell," *The Republic of Letters: Essays on Various Writers*, pp. 89-123. New York: Alfred A. Knopf, 1955.

373. ——————(ed.). *The Portable Johnson and Boswell*. Viking Portable Library. New York: Viking Press, 1947.

374. KRUTCH, J. W. "The Last Boswell Paper," *SRL*, XXXIV (July 21, 1951), 13-15. A parody. Reprinted in item 253.

375. KUNITZ, Stanley J., and Howard Haycroft (eds.). *British Authors Before 1800: A Biographical Dictionary*, pp. 50-52. New York: Wilson, 1952.

376. L., A. "Boswellian Personages," *NQ*, III (Ser. 2; April 25, 1857), 330-331. Reply to item 174.

377. L., B. H. "Boswell's Last London Residence," *NQ*, I (Ser. 9; June 11, 1898), 466. No tablet marks the house in which Boswell died. See items 142 and 623.

378. LALOU, René. "Boswell en Italie et en Corse," *Revue de Paris*, LXIII (1956), 49-55.

379. LANE, William C., and Nina E. Browne (eds.). "Portraits of James Boswell," *American Library As-*

sociation Portrait Index, p. 167. Washington: Government Printing Office, 1906.

379.1. LASCELLES, Mary. "Notions and Facts: Johnson and Boswell on Their Travels," *Johnson, Boswell, and Their Circle; Essays Presented to L. F. Powell in Honour of His Eighty-fourth Birthday,* pp. 215-229. Oxford University Press, 1965.

380. LAYARD, G. S. "Johnson's Boswell," *Universal Rev.,* VI (Aug., 1890), 535.

381. LEE, Sir Sidney. *Principles of Biography,* pp. 42-49. The Leslie Stephen Lecture, 1911. Cambridge University Press, 1911. Boswell's merit and his methods.

382. LEIGH, R. A. "Boswell and Rousseau," *MLR,* XLVII (July, 1952), 289-318. Explains why Boswell sought great men.

383. LETTS, M., and William Jaggard. "Boswell's Journal," *NQ,* CLXXVIII (Feb. 3, 1940), 89. Reply to item 483.

384. LEWIS, W. S. "The Young Waterman," *VQR,* XXV (1949), 66-73. An adventure in the *Life.*

385. LIBRA. "Boswell and Anna Seward," *Gentleman's Mag.,* LXIV (April, 1794), 311-312. Boswell's controversy with her.

385.1. LIEBERT, Herman W. "Boswell's 'Life of Johnson,' 1791," *American NQ,* I (1962), 6-7. Discusses variants of the first edition.

386. "Life of Boswell," *Blackwood's Mag.,* CLXXXV (Feb. 1909), 233-251. Discusses item 399.

GENERAL STUDIES

387.   LINDSAY, Norman A. W. "The New Boswell," *Bulletin*, LXXII (Feb., 1951), 2.

388.   LOCHHEAD, Marion. *The Scots Household in the Eighteenth Century*, pp. 361-363. Edinburgh: Murray Press, 1948.

388.1. LOCKHART, J. G. "Croker's Edition of Boswell," *Quarterly Rev.*, XLVI (Nov., 1831), 1-46. See item 399.

389.   *"London Journal, 1762-1763," Harper's Mag.*, CCI (Nov., 1950), 28-39. Pre-publication excerpts.

390.   LONGAKER, John M. "Boswell's *Life of Johnson*," *English Biography of the Eighteenth Century*, pp. 407-476. Philadelphia: University of Pennsylvania Press, 1931. Includes bibliography.

391.   LONSDALE, Roger. "Dr. Burney and the Integrity of Boswell's Quotations," *Papers of the Bibliographical Society of America*, LIII (1959), 327-331.

392.   LOWRY, Walker. "James Boswell, Scots Advocate and English Barrister," *Stanford Law Rev.*, II (1950), 471-495. The law Boswell had to know in order to practice.

393.   LUCAS, Frank L. *The Search for Good Sense; Four 18th Century Characters: Johnson, Chesterfield, Boswell, Goldsmith*, pp. 177-282. London: Cassell; New York: Macmillan, 1958.

394.   LUCAS, St. John. "Vagabond Impressions: Rousseau and Boswell," *Blackwood's Mag.*, CCXII (Nov., 1922), 631-638. Boswell in France and Corsica.

395.   LUCAS, Samuel. "James Boswell," *Eminent Men and*

Popular Books, pp. 231-264. London: N. p., 1859.

395.1.   LUSTIG, Irma S. "Boswell on Politics in the *Life of Johnson," PMLA,* LXXX (1965), 387-393.

395.2.   _____. "Boswell's Literary Criticism in the *Life of Samuel Johnson," SEL,* VI (1966), 529-541.

396.   LYALL, Alexander. "The Case of Dr. Memis versus Managers of the Aberdeen Royal Infirmary," *Medical History,* IV (1960), 32-48.

397.   LYND, Robert. "Boswell," *Dr. Johnson and Company,* pp. 43-82. London: Hodder, 1927; New York: Doubleday, 1928.

398.   _____. "Boswell," *Essays on Life and Literature,* pp. 71-86. New York: E. P. Dutton and Co., 1951.

399.   MACAULAY, Thomas B. "Essay on Boswell's 'Life of Johnson,'" *Edinburgh Rev.,* LIV (Sept., 1831), 1-38. See also Macaulay's essay on Samuel Johnson in *The Encyclopedia Brittanica,* Seventh Edition (1842). These two articles influenced public opinion of Boswell and Johnson until after the turn of the century. The review may be found in almost all of the collected works of Lord Macaulay. For replies, see the index under Macaulay and especially items 228, 386, 427, 433, and 467.

400.   MACCARTHY, B. G. "James Boswell' A Problem," *Studies,* XXXVI (1947), 319-325.

401.   MACCARTHY, Desmond. "Boswell," *Criticism,* pp. 30-35. New York: G. P. Putnam's Sons, 1932.

402.   MACLAURIN, C. "Dr. Johnson," *Mere Mortals,* pp. 17-39. New York: Doran, 1925; reprinted in *Post*

Mortem of Mere Mortals, pp. 17-39. New York: Sun Dial Press, 1940.

403.   MacPHAIL, Andrew. "Johnson's Life of Boswell," *QR*, CCLIII (July, 1929), 42-73. The relationship of Boswell and Johnson.

404.   MacPHAIL, J. R. "James Boswell, Esq.," *Cornhill Mag.*, LXIII (July, 1927), 31-43.

405.   MACRAY, W. D. "A Note on Boswell's 'Life of Johnson,'" *NQ*, XII (Ser. 5; Oct. 11, 1879), 285. Johnson's use of the Bible. See item 549.

406.   MAGILL, Frank N. (ed.). *Cyclopedia of World Authors*, pp. 118-121. New York: Harper and Brothers, 1958.

407.   MAIS, Stuart P. B. "James Boswell," *Why Should We Read*, pp. 35-37. London: Richards, 1921.

408.   "The Making of Boswell's 'Johnson,'" *TLS*, Feb. 6, 1930, pp. 85-86. Editions of Boswell's *Life*. See items 121 and 302.

409.   MALLORY, George. *Boswell the Biographer*. London: Smith Elder, 1912. A character sketch.

410.   MARTIN, Samuel. *An Epistle in Verse, Occasioned by the Death of James Boswell, Esquire, of Auchinleck. Addressed to the Rev. Dr. T. D. by the Rev. Samuel Martin, Minister of Monimail*. Edinburgh: Printed by Mundell and Son, R. Bank Close; London: Sold by Messrs. Vernor and Hood and Allen and West, 1795. Reprinted in a facsimile edition, ed. Robert F. Metzdorf. Hamden, Conn.: Shoe String Press, 1952.

410.1. MASTIGOPHORUS. "Mr. Boswell and Miss Seward,"

Gentleman's Mag., LXIV (Feb., 1794), 121. The Boswell-Seward controversy.

411.   MAXWELL, Patrick. "Boswell's 'Johnson,'" *NQ*, I (Ser. 9; May 14, 1898), 385-386. Greek inscription on the St. Paul's monument to Johnson. See items 412, 436, 554, and 555.

412.   ————, *NQ*, I (Ser. 9; June 4, 1898), 452. Defends his earlier remarks. See items 411, 436, 554, and 555.

412.1. McADAM, E. L., Jr. *Johnson and Boswell: A Survey of Their Writings.* Riverside Studies in Literature Boston: Houghton, Mifflin, Co., 1969.

412.2. McCOLLUM, John I., Jr. "The Indebtedness of James Boswell to Edmond Malone," *New Rambler*, I (Ser. C; June, 1966), 29-45.

413.   McCUTCHEON, Roger P. "Johnson, Boswell, and Gold smith," *Eighteenth-Century English Literature*, pp. 83-87. Oxford University Press, 1949.

414.   ————. "Johnson and Boswell Today," *Addresses Made before the Friends of the Howard-Tilton Memorial Library of Tulane University*, pp. 16-28. New Orleans: N. P., 1944.

415.   McELDERRY, B. R. "Boswell in 1790-1791: Two Unpublished Comments," *NQ*, CCVII (July, 1962), 266-268. Boswell and Mrs. Elizabeth Montagu.

416.   McKINLAY, Robert. "Boswell's Fugitive Pieces," *Records of the Glasgow Bibliographical Society*, VIII (1930), 64-77.

416.1. McLAREN, Moray. *Corsica Boswell.* London: Secker and Warburg, 1966.

417.   ————. "Dr. Johnson's Island," *New Statesman*, XLV (Jan. 24, 1953), 88. Visit to a Scottish island with Boswell.

418.   ————. *The Highland Jaunt: A Study of James Boswell and Samuel Johnson upon Their Highland and Hebridean Tour of 1773*. London: Jarrolds, 1954. Mainly concerned with Boswell.

419.   ————. "James Boswell," *The Wisdom of the Scots*, pp. 244-288. London: Michael Joseph, 1961. Comment on Boswell and his journals.

419.1.   MEIER, W. "Johnson and Boswell," *Frendesgabe für Eduard Korrodi*. Zurich, 1945.

420.   "Memoir of James Boswell, Esq.," *Literary Magazine and American Register*, I (1804), 224-238.

421.   MERRITT, E. Percival. "Piozzi on Boswell and Johnson," *HLN*, II (April, 1926), 104-111. Annotations in Mrs. Piozzi's copies of *Hebrides* and the *Life*.

422.   METCALF, John C. "Boswell's Methods and Materials," *The Stream of English Biography*, pp. 21-26. New York and London: The Century Co., 1930.

422.1.   METZDORF, Robert F. "A New Wordsworth Letter," *MLN*, LIX (March, 1944), 168-170. Wordsworth on Boswell.

422.2.   MIDDLETON, Michael. "James Boswell: A Familiar Stranger," *Studio*, CLXIII (Feb., 1962), 48-51.

423.   MILNES, Richard Moncton (Baron Houghton). "Boswelliana," *Philobiblon Society Miscellanies*, II (1856), 1-27. See items 133 and 600.

424. _____. *Boswelliana: The Commonplace Book of James Boswell. With a Memoir and Annotations by the Rev. Charles Rogers... and Introductory Remarks by the Rgt. Hon. Lord Houghton.* London: Grampian Club, 1874.

424.1. "Mr. Boswell Comes to Town," *TLS*, Oct. 19, 1967, p. 1000. See item 369.1.

425. MITCHELL, W. Fraser. "A Reminiscence of Boswell: Lord Gardenstone's Lawrence Kirk Projects," *University of Edinburgh Journal*, VI (1933-1934), 232-241.

426. MORGAN, H. A. "Boswell on the Grand Tour," *New Rambler*, June, 1961, pp. 14-19.

427. _____. "Boswell and Macaulay," *Contemporary Rev.*, CXCIII (1958), 27-29. Comments on item 399.

428. MORGAN, Lee. "Boswell's Portrait of Goldsmith," *Studies in Honor of John C. Hodges and Alvin Thaler*, pp. 67-76. Knoxville: University of Tennessee Press, 1961. Finds Boswell abusive of Goldsmith.

429. MORLEY, Christopher. "The Boswell Papers: A Legend of Impropriety," *SRL*, XXXIII (Oct. 7, 1950), 11-14. See item 3.

430. _____. "A Supper of Larks," *SRL*, XIX (Dec. 3, 1938), 13, 26. Boswell, Johnson, and Mrs. Piozzi.

431. _____. "Two Days We Celebrate," *Mince Pie; Adventures on the Sunny Side of Grub Street*, pp. 117-131. New York: Doubleday-Doran, 1919; *Essays*, pp. 275-288. New York: Doubleday-Doran, 1928; *Essays Light and Serious*, pp. 34-45, ed. Walter F. Langford. Toronto: Longmans, Green Co., 1954.

431.1. Morris, J. N. "Being Boswell," *Versions of the Self: Studies in Autobiography from John Bunyan to John Stuart Mill*. New York: Basic Books, 1966.

431.2. —————. "The Book of Moments," *Versions of the Self: Studies in Autobiography from John Bunyan to John Stuart Mill*, pp. 171-188. New York: Basic Books, 1966.

432. Mossner, Ernest. "Dr. Johnson *in Partibus Infidelium?*" *MLN*, LXIII (Dec., 1948), 516-519. Boswell's house.

433. Mount, C. B. "Macaulay on Boswell," *NQ*, IV (Ser. 8; Aug. 12, 1893), 126. See items 178 and 399.

433.1. M——s. "Controversy Closed," *Gentleman's Mag.*, LXIV (Feb., 1794), 120. Boswell and Anna Seward.

434. Muir, Marie. *Dear Mrs. Boswell*. London: Macmillan, 1954. Fictitious account of Boswell's marriage.

435. Murdock, Harold. *Earl Percy Dines Abroad, A Boswellian Episode*. Boston: Houghton-Mifflin Co., 1924.

435.1. Murray, John. "Boswell's 'Johnson,'" *NQ*, I (Ser. 9; May 21, 1898), 409. See items 411, 412, 554, and 555.

436. Murray, John. "Boswell and the Scots Magazine," *Scots Mag.*, XXXIII (New ser.; 1940).

437. —————. "Notes on Johnson's Movements in Scotland. Suggested Attributions to Boswell in the *Caledonian Mercury*," *NQ*, CLXXVIII (1940), 3-5; 182-185. Lists articles supposedly written by Boswell.

438. ―――――. "Some Civil Cases of James Boswell, 1772-1774," *Juridical Rev.*, LII (1940), 222-251. The extent of Boswell's legal practice.

439. MYFANNY. "The Poet Bacon," *NQ*, IV (Ser. 1; Dec. 27, 1851), 507. Suggests the Rev. Phannel Bacon. See items 179 and 473.

439.1. N., J. [John Nichols] *Gentleman's Mag.*, LXIII (Jan., 1793), 19. Comments on the *Life*.

440. ―――――. "Johnsonian Verses," *Gentleman's Mag.*, LXI (May, 1791), 396. Poems in the *Life*.

441. ―――――. "More Last Words of Dr. Johnson," *Gentleman's Mag.*, LXI (June, 1791), 499-500.

442. N., L. "Boswell's Johnson," *NQ*, XII (Ser. 1; Oct. 20, 1855), 304. Asks for the number of editions of the *Life* Boswell supervised. See item 221.

442.1. N., N. "Remarks on the Life of Boswell," *Monthly Mag.*, XVI (Sept., 1803), 98-99. Reply to item 311.1.

443. N., S. "Boswell to Reynolds, 1775," *NQ*, CLXXVI (June 3, 1939), 390; (June 17, 1939), 427. A portrait's engraved inscription. See item 297.

444. NAUGHTON, A. E. A. "James Boswell with Rousseau, 1764," *MLF*, XVIII (1933), 47-54.

445. NEWMARK, Leo. "News for Bibliophiles," *Nation*, XCVII (Sept. 11, 1913), 232. An incomplete German translation of the *Life* in 1797, made from the second edition.

446. NEWTON, A. Edward. "James Boswell—His Book," *The Amenities of Book-Collecting and Kindred*

Affections, pp. 145-185. Boston: Atlantic Monthly Press, 1918. Johnson and Boswell.

447. _____(Intro.). *Reproduction of Some of the Original Proof Sheets of Boswell's Life of Johnson.* Buffalo: Privately Printed for R. B. Adam, 1923. See item 516.

448. NICHOLS, John. *Illustrations of the Literary History of the 18th Century*, VII (1848), 300-383. 8 vols. London: Nichols, Son, and Bentley, 1817-1858. Correspondence and opinions of Boswell.

449. _____. *Literary Anecdotes of the Eighteenth Century*, II, 400-404; VII, 38, and see Nichols's index for further references. 9 vols. London: Nichols, Son, and Bentley, 1812-1815.

450. NICOLL, W. Robertson, "The Six Best Biographies," *A Bookman's Letters*, pp. 17-25. London: Hodder and Stoughton, 1915.

451. NICOLSON, Harold. "The Boswell Formula, 1791," *The Development of English Biography*, pp. 87-109. London: L. and Virginia Woolf, 1927; New York: Harcourt, Brace and Co., 1928. Boswell's personality and his work.

452. NOLAN, Paul T. "A Shakespeare Idol in America," *Mississippi Quarterly*, XII (1959), 64-74. Boswell's attitude toward Shakespeare.

452.1. NOYES, Charles E. "Samuel Johnson: Student of Hume," *University of Mississippi Studies in English*, III (1962), 91-94. Boswell's estimate of the subject.

453. O., J. "Boswell's 'Johnson,'" *NQ*, I (Ser. 2; May 24, 1856), 407-408. Two queries and a note.

453.1. "Obituary of Mrs. Gastrell," *Gentleman's Mag.*, LXI (Dec., 1791), 1159. See item 139.1.

454. O'NEILL, Edward H. *A History of American Biography*, pp. 6, 291-292. Philadelphia: University of Pennsylvania Press, 1935.

454.1. OSBORN, James M. *'By Appointment to His Majesty Biographer of Samuel Johnson, LL. D.' For the Annual Dinner of the Johnsonians in Celebration of Dr. Johnson's Two Hundred and Fifty-fifth Birthday 18 September 1964 with Facsimiles of the Originals in the Yale University Library.* New Haven: Yale University Press, 1964. A cancel in the second edition of the *Life*.

454.2. OSGOOD, Charles G. "An American Boswell," *PULC*, V (1944), 85-91.

455. ————. "Lady Phillipina Knight and Her Boswell," *PULC*, IV (Feb.-April, 1943), 37-49. Lady Knight's annotations in her daughter's copy of the *Life*.

456. "Opinions of Persons and Books, By Dr. Johnson and Mr. Boswell," *Gentleman's Mag.*, LV (Dec., 1785), 970-971. On Forbes, Beattie, Swift, Garrick, and Reynolds.

457. P., L. G. "Croker's Boswell," *NQ*, II (Ser. 1; Nov. 2, 1850), 373. The Earl of Shelburne in Croker's edition of the *Life*.

458. P., W. "Johnsoniana," *NQ*, VII (Ser. 1; April 2, 1853), 328-329. An unpublished letter from Boswell to David Garrick.

459. PARR, S. "Dr. Johnson and Dr. Priestley," *Gentleman's Mag.*, LXV (March, 1795), 179-181. Errors in the *Life*. See items 269, 312, and 534.

460.   PARSONS, Mrs. Clement. "Boswell's Tact," *Life and Letters*, III (Dec., 1929), 503-513.

461.   PARTINGTON, Wilfrid. "Boswell: His Life, Loves, and Letters," *Bookman's Journal*, XI (Feb., 1925), 200-205.

462.   PEARSON, Hesketh. "Boswell as Artist," *Cornhill Mag.*, CXLVI (Dec., 1932), 704-711. Boswell's methods in biography.

463.   _____. *Johnson and Boswell: The Story of Their Lives*. London: William Heinemann; New York: Harper and Brothers, 1958. Their lives, together and apart.

464.   _____. *Ventilations: Being Biographical Asides*, pp. 11-20, *et passim*. London and Philadelphia: J. B. Lippincott Co., 1930. Boswell's veracity.

465.   _____, and Hugh Kingsmill [H. K. Lunn]. *Skye High: The Record of a Tour Through Scotland in the Wake of Samuel Johnson and James Boswell*. London: Hamish Hamilton, 1937. A series of dialogs in the Boswellian manner.

465.1.   PETTIT, H. "Boswell and Young's Night Thoughts," *NQ*, CCX (Jan., 1965), 21.

466.   PHELAN, Paul J. "How Truly Catholic was Boswell?" *America*, LXIV (Oct., 1940), 47-48.

467.   PHILALETHES. *Boswell Again*. London and Edinburgh: N. p., 1878. Reply to item 399.

467.1.   PHILANTHROPUS. "Remarks on Boswell," *Gentleman's Mag.*, (April, 1786), 295-296. Comments on *Hebrides*.

468.   PHILLIPSON, J. S. "Boswell Rediscovered—A Decade

Later," *Catholic Library World*, XXXI (May, 1960), 491-496.

469.   PINDAR, Peter [John Wolcot]. *Bozzy and Piozzi, or, the British Biographers: a Town Eclogue*, Londdon: G. Kearsley and W. Foster, 1786. Heroic couplets dealing with the trivialities of Boswell and Piozzi.

470.   _____. *A Poetical and Congratulatory Epsitle to James Boswell, Esq., on His Journal of A Tour to the Hebrides*. London: N. p., 1786.

470.1.   _____. *The Works of Peter Pindar, Esq.* 5 vols. 2nd edition. London: Walker, 1812. Contains items 469 and 470.

471.   PLEADWELL, Frank L. "Lord Mountstuart—Boswell's *Maecenas*," *American Collector*, V (1928), 233-241. Letters of Boswell.

471.1.   *A Poetical Epistle from the Ghost of Dr. Johnson to His Four Friends: Rev. Mr. Strahan, Boswell, Mrs. Piozzi, and Courtenay*. London, 1786.

472.   POCOCK, G. N. "Lexicographer's Chair," *Little Room*, pp. 102-109. New York: E. P. Dutton and Co., 1926.

473.   PORCULUS. "Bacon a Poet," *NQ*, IV (Ser. 1; Dec. 27, 1851), 506-507. See items 179, 334, and 439.

474.   POTTLE, Frederick A. "A Blank in Boswell's Journal," *NQ*, CLXXVII (July 29, 1939), 80; (Oct. 28, 1939), 319-320. See item 564.

475.   _____. "Boswelliana: Two Attributions," *NQ*, CXLVII (Oct. 18, 1924), 281; (Nov. 22, 1924),

375. Asks for information on 'Observations on *The Minor*' and one other piece.

476. _____. "Boswellian Myths," *NQ*, CXLIX (July 4, 1925), 4-6. Boswell and Mrs. Rudd and Ireland.

477. _____. "Boswellian Notes," *NQ*, CXLIX (Aug. 15, 1925), 113-114. Asks if Boswell wrote 'Reflections on the...Bankrupticies in Scotland.'

478. _____. *Boswell and the Girl from Botany Bay.* New York: Viking Press, 1937. Reprinted in Alexander Woollcott, *Woollcott's Second Reader.* New York: Viking Press, 1937. See item 135.

478.1. _____. "Boswell as Icarus," *Restoration and Eighteenth Century Literature*, pp. 389-406, ed. Carroll Camden. University of Chicago Press for Rice University, 1963.

479. _____. "Boswell in Love: His Private Papers and Correspondence with Zélide," *Atlantic Mo.*, CLXXXIX (1952), 34-43. A preview of item 4.

480. _____. "Boswell Revalued," *Literary Views: Critical and Historical Essays*, pp. 79-91, ed. Carroll Camden. University of Chicago Press for Rice University Semi-Centennial Series, 1964.

481. _____. "Boswell's Corsica," *YULG*, I (June, 1926), 21-22.

481.1. _____. "Boswell's Executors," *TLS*, Nov. 3, 1927, p. 790.

482. _____. "Boswell's 'Life of Johnson,'" *NQ*, CLXXVIII (1940), 50-51. Reply to item 313: Pottle finds no full translations to 1940.

483. _____."Boswell's Journal: Source of Quotation Wanted," *NQ*, CLXXVIII (Jan. 20, 1940), 44. See item 383 for reply.

484. _____. (ed.). "Boswell's London Journal," *Omnibook*, XIII (March, 1951), 1-34. Excerpts, with an introduction (pp. 1-5) by Pottle.

485. _____. "Boswell's 'Matrimonial Thought,' " *NQ*, CXLVII (Oct. 18, 1924), 283. Reply to item 231.

486. _____. "Boswell's 'Miss W_____T,' " *NQ*, CXLVIII (Jan. 31, 1925), 80. Asks identity of this lady is Boswell's letters to Temple.

487. _____. "Boswell's 'Observations on *The Minor*,' " *BNYPL*, XXIX (1925), 3-6. Boswell's first separate publication.

488. _____. "Boswell's Shorthand," *TLS*, July 28, 1932, p. 545. Cryptic writing in the Journals. See item 110.

489. _____. "Boswell's University Education," *Johnson, Boswell, and Their Circle: Essays Presented to L. F. Powell in Honour of His Eighty-fourth Birthday*, pp. 230-253. Oxford University Press, 1965.

490. _____. "Bozzy and Yorick," *Blackwood's Mag.*, CCXVII (March, 1925), 297-313. Boswell's meetings with Sterne.

491. _____. "Bozzy Was a Bold Young Blade: The Story of His Lady Mackintosh Episode Based on Unpublished Material," *NYTBR*, Aug. 23, 1925, pp. 1, 13. A youthful experience.

492. _____. "The Dark Hints of Sir John Hawkins and

Boswell Concerning Johnson," *MLN*, LVI (1941), 325-329. Revised and enlarged in *New Light on Dr. Johnson*, ed. F. W. Hilles, pp. 153-162. New Haven: Yale University Press, 1959. Johnson's "sexual irregularities" in early life.

493. —————. "His Own Boswell," *SRL*, V (July 20, 1929), 1187-1188. Boswell and Zélide.

494. —————. "The Incredible Boswell," *Blackwood's Mag.*, CCXVIII (Aug., 1925), 149-165. Boswell's MS copies of his contributions to the *London Chronicle*.

495. —————. "James Boswell, Journalist," *The Age of Johnson: Essays Presented to Chauncey Brewster Tinker*, pp. 15-25. New Haven: Yale University Press, 1949. Boswell's techniques.

496. —————. "James Boswell the Younger," *NQ*, CXLIX (July 18, 1925), 49. Gives date of birth of Boswell's son; place of birth unknown.

497. —————. "The Life of Boswell," *Yale Rev.*, XXXV (1946), 445-460. Boswell's self-revelations in his journals and elsewhere.

498. —————. "Malone and Boswell," *SRL*, VI (Aug. 24, 1929), 74. Boswell's journals.

499. —————. "'A North Briton Extraordinary': Boswell and Corsica," *NQ*, CXLVII (Oct. 11, 1924), 259-261; (Dec. 6, 1924), 403-404. Queries authorship.

499.1. —————. "Notes on the Importance of Private Legal Documents for the Writing of Biography," *Proceedings of the American Philosophical Society*, CVI (1962), 327-334.

500. ————. "The Part Played by Horace Walpole and James Boswell in the Quarrel between Rousseau and Hume," *PQ*, IV (Oct., 1925), 351-363. See also *PQ*, V (April, 1926), 185, for *errata* in the above corrected. Letters and a poem by Boswell and Walpole. Revised and expanded in *Horace Walpole: Writer, Politician, and Connoisseur. Essays on the 250th Anniversary of Walpole's Birth*, pp. 255-291, ed. Warren H. Smith. New Haven: Yale University Press, 1967.

501. ————. "Portraits of James Boswell," *NQ*, CLII (Jan. 29, 1927), 80-81. Asks whereabouts of six paintings.

502. ————. "The Power of Memory in Boswell and Scott," *Essays on the Eighteenth Century Presented to David Nichol Smith in Honour of His 70th Birthday*, pp. 168-189. Oxford University Press, 1945. Memory + imagination = Boswell.

503. ————. "Printer's Copy in the Eighteenth Century," *Papers of the Bibliographical Society of America*, XXVII (1933), 65-73. Boswell's manuscripts.

504. ————. "Queries from Boswell," *NQ*, CLXXV (Sept. 17, 1938), 208. Boswell's journals.

505. ————. "Queries on Boswell's 'Johnson,'" *NQ*, CLXXXI (Dec. 6, 1941), 317. Six questions.

506. ————. "Three New Legal Ballads by James Boswell," *Juridical Rev.*, XXXVII (1925), 201-211. Three poems, one never published, attributed to Boswell.

506.1. ————, and Charles H. Bennett. "Boswell and

Mrs. Piozzi," *MP*, XXXIX (May, 1942), 421-430. Boswell and Piozzi as competitors.

507.   POWELL, L. F. "The Anonymous Designations in Boswell's 'Journal of a Tour to the Hebrides' and Their Identification," *Edinburgh Bibliographical Society Transactions*, II (1938-1945), 353-371.

507.1.   _____. "A Boswellian Identification," *TLS*, March 30, 1967, p. 274.

508.   _____. "Boswell's Original Journal of His Tour to the Hebrides and the Printed Version," *Essays and Studies by Members of the English Association*, XXIII (1938), 58-69.

509.   _____. "Boswell's 'Hebrides,' 31 August," *NQ*, CLXXXIV (March 27, 1943), 202. A book purchased by Boswell.

510.   _____. "Boswell's 'Life of Johnson,'" *NQ*, CLXXXII (March 7-May 9, 1942), 136, 147, 176-177, 206, 209, 235, 260; CLXXXIII (1942), 17; CLXXXIV (Jan. 16, 1943), 46; (April 24, 1943), 257-258; (May 22, 1943), 318; CLXXXV (Dec. 18, 1943), 379. A long list of queries. For partial replies, see items 98 and 99.

511.   _____. "'The History of St. Kilda'," *RES*, XVI (Jan., 1940), 44-53. Boswell's and Johnson's opinions of Macaulay's book.

512.   _____. "The New Birkbeck-Hill," *TLS*, Aug. 3, 1933, p. 525. Eleven queries on items in Hill's edition of the *Life*, IV.

513.   _____. "The Revision of Dr. Birkbeck Hill's Boswell," *Johnson and Boswell Revised by Themselves and Others*, pp. 53-66. A Johnson Club

Paper for March 14, 1928. Oxford University Press, 1928.

513.1.   ————. *A Task Ended*. Lichfield Johnson Society, 1950.

514.   PRICE, Cecil. "Meetings with Boswell," *TLS*, March 8, 1947, p. 103. Boswell's contemporaries.

515.   PRITCHETT, Victor S. "Boswell's London," *Books in General*, pp. 75-80. New York: Harcourt, Brace Co., 1953.

516.   "Proofsheets of Boswell's 'Johnson,'" *TLS*, Jan. 17, 1924, p. 44. R. B. Adams's reprint of these sheets. See item 447.

516.1.   PROTOPLASTIDES. "Critique on Boswell," *Gentleman's Mag.*, LXIV (July, 1794), 623-625. Comments on the *Life*, first edition.

517.   ————. "Remarks on Dr. Johnson: Grammatical Strictures," *Gentleman's Mag.*, LXV (Jan., 1795), 6-8. Points out errors in the *Life*.

517.1.   "Publications Relating to the Douglas Cause," *Scots Mag.*, XXIX (July, 1767), 338-344. Comments on Boswell's *Dorando*.

518.   PUDNEY, John. *Low Life; Verses. Drawings by James Boswell*. London: Bodley Head, 1947.

519.   Q. "Mr. Boswell's Gong," *Gentleman's Mag.*, LV (Nov., 1785), 877. Zany activities in London.

520.   QUENNELL, Peter. "James Boswell," *The Profane Virtues: Four Studies of the Eighteenth Century*, pp. 1-63. New York: Viking Press, 1945. An adapted version of item 522.

521. _____. "Books in General," *New Statesman and Nation*, XXXII (Dec. 21, 1946), 465.

522. _____. "Boswell's Progress," *Horizon*, VI (Dec., 1942), 394-403; VII (June, 1943), 422-430; VIII (July, 1943), 45-54. See item 520.

522.1. QUERIST. "To the Man of Letters and to the Man of Fashion," *Gentleman's Mag.*, LXI (July, 1791), 631. Defense of the *Life*, probably written by Boswell himself.

522.2. R., E. R. "Boswell's 'Tour,'" *Gentleman's Mag.*, LVI (Sept., 1786), 730.

523. R., J. B. "Memoirs of James Boswell, Esq.," *Gentleman's Mag.*, LXV (June, 1795), 487-489. An account of Boswell's literary contributions.

524. R., V. "Johnson, Boswell, and Grattan," *NQ*, CLXXXI (Nov. 15, 1941), 273. An omission in the Hill-Powell *Life*, IV, 317.

524.1. RADER, R. W. "Literary Form in Factual Narrative: The Example of Boswell's *Johnson*," *Essays in Eighteenth Century Biography*, ed. P. B. Daghlian. Bloomington: Indiana University Press, 1968.

524.2. RAE, Thomas I., and William Beattie. "Boswell and the Advocate's Library," *Johnson, Boswell, and Their Circle; Essays Presented to L. F. Powell in Honour of His Eighty-fourth Birthday*, pp. 254-267. Oxford University Press, 1965.

525. RAIT, Sir R. S. "Boswell and Lockhart," *Essays by Divers Hands*, XII (1933), 105-127.

526. RALEIGH, Sir Walter. "Johnson without Boswell,"

Six Essays on Johnson, pp. 40ff. Oxford University Press, 1910. Boswell as biographer.

527. RALLI, Augustus J. "Boswell," *Critiques*, pp. 187-205. London: Longmans, Green and Co., 1927.

528. ───────. *Westminster Rev.*, CLXXIX (March, 1913), 270-283. Boswell's character and the *Life*.

529. RAMSAY, James. "Boswell's First Criminal Case: John Reid—Sheep Stealer," *Juridical Rev.*, L (1938), 315-321. A history of the case.

530. RAWLINSON, Robert. "The True Solution," *NQ*, X (Ser. 1; Dec. 9, 1854), 472. See items 222, 236, and 237. The mathematics problem.

530.1. REED, Joseph W., Jr. "Boswell and the Major," *Kenyon Rev.*, XXVIII (1966), 161-184. Boswell, Major James G. Semple, and Edmund Burke. Also printed as "Boswell and After," *English Biography of the Nineteenth Century: 1801-1838*, pp. 3-26. New Haven: Yale University Press, 1966.

531. REEVES, A. S. Frere. "Boswell's Journal," *TLS*, April 25. 1936, p. 928. Corrects a *Hebrides* reviewer.

531.1. REIBERG, Rufus. "James Boswell's Personal Correspondence: The Dramatized Quest for Identity," *The Familiar Letter in the Eighteenth Century*, pp. 244-268, ed. Howard Anderson, Philip B. Daghlian, and Irvin Ehrenpreis. University of Kansas Press, 1966.

532. REID, Benjamin L. "Johnson's Life of Boswell," *Kenyon Rev.*, XVIII (1956), 546-575. The same in Reid's *The Long Boy, and Others*, pp. 1-30. Athens: University of Georgia Press, 1969.

533. REILLY, Joseph J. "Bozzy: The Man Who Made Johnson," *Dear Prue's Husband and Other People*, pp. 68-78. New York: Macmillan Co., 1932. Calls Boswell an "irrepressible, sophomoric, irritating sprig of North British lairdliness, James Boswell—a genius."

533.1. "Reply to the Defender of Boswell's Journal," *Gentleman's Mag.*, LVI (May, 1786), 386-388. Concerns *Hebrides*.

533.2. "Review of Dugald Stewart's *Life of William Robertson*," *Edinburgh Rev.*, II (April, 1803), 229-249. See pp. 234-235 for comment of Boswell.

534. "Review of 'Remarks on the *Journal of a Tour to the Hebrides with Dr. Samuel Johnson, LL. D.*,' in a Letter to James Boswell, Esq., 1785," *Gentleman's Mag.*, LV (Dec., 1785), 978. Boswell's character. See items 269, 312, and 459.

534.1. REWA, Michael. "Boswell's 'Life of Johnson,' IV, 420-421," *NQ*, CCXII (1967), 411-412. William Hamilton's comment on Johnson's death.

535. RICHARDSON, J. J. "Bozzy," *Manchester Quarterly*, XXVIII (1909), 234-245.

536. ROBERTS, Sydney Castle. "Discovery of James Boswell," *Discovery*, I (New ser.; Aug., 1938), 252-254.

537. _____. *Doctor Johnson in Cambridge. Essays in Boswellian Imitation.* London: G.P. Putnam's Sons, 1922.

538. _____. *Dr. Johnson and Others*, pp. 24-39. Cambridge University Press, 1958.

539.   ————. "More Boswell Letters," *TLS*, Jan. 1, 1954, p. 16. Sixty letters from Boswell to his cousin, Robert Boswell.

540.   ————. *The Story of Doctor Johnson, Being an Introduction to Boswell's Life.* Cambridge University Press, 1919.

541.   ROBERTS, W. "Hoppner and Porteus," *TLS*, July 5, 1934, p. 476.

542.   ROBINSON, Frederic W. *A Commentary and Questionnaire on a Journal of a Tour to the Hebrides-Boswell.* London: N. p., 1929.

543.   ROGERS, Charles. *Memoir, Prefixed to Boswelliana.* London: Grampian Club, 1874.

544.   ROMEIN, Jan. *De Biographie een Inleiding*, pp. 39-40. Amsterdam: Uitgeverij Ploegsma, 1946. Boswell established a norm for English biography.

545.   ROSE, Kenneth. "Portrait the Second: Boswell Meets Johnson," *Georgiana: Seven Portraits*, pp. 10-15. London: Muller, 1947. A short play.

545.1.   ROSS, Ian. "Boswell in Search of a Father? Or a Subject," *Review of English Literature*, V (Jan., 1964), 19-34. Boswell and Lord Kames.

546.   ROTH, G. "James Boswell and Jean Jacques Rousseau," *London Mercury*, VIII (Sept., 1923), 493-506.

547.   ROUGHEAD, William. *Rascals Revived.* London: Cassells, 1940.

548.   ROWLANDSON, Thomas, and Samuel Collings. *Pic-

turesque Beauties of Boswell. London: E. Jackson and G. Kearsley, 1786. Twenty caricatures drawn from the text of Boswell's *Hebrides.*

549.   RULE, Frederick. "A Note on Boswell's 'Life of Johnson,'" *NQ*, XII (Ser. 5; Nov. 29, 1879), 433. Replies to item 405.

550.   RUSSELL, A. J. "Unpardonable Interruption," *Bellman*, XXIV (June 15, 1918), 664-665.

551.   RUSSELL, Sir Charles. "Johnson, Gibbon, and Boswell," *Fortnightly Rev.*, CXIX (May, 1926), 629-635. Boswell's dislike of Gibbon.

552.   RUSSELL, Constance. "Boswell and Erskine," *NQ*, VI (Ser. 7; Dec. 15, 1888), 473. See item 572.

552.1.   RYSKAMP, Charles. "Boswell and Walter James; Goethe and Daniel Malthus," *Eighteenth Century Studies in Honor of Donald F. Hyde*, ed. W. H. Bond, pp. 207-229. New York: Grolier Club, 1970.

552.2.   S., B. B. "Dr. Johnson's Letter on His Mother's Death," *Gentleman's Mag.*, LXIV (March, 1794), 196. Comments on the *Life*, second edition.

553.   S., E. L. "Boswell's Ride to Tyburn," *NQ*, IV (Ser. 3; Sept. 5, 1863), 186. Boswell and the murderer, Hackman. See item 230.

553.1.   S., G. "Boswell," *Gentleman's Mag.*, LXIV (March, 1794), 197-198. Comments on the *Life*.

554.   S., J. "Boswell's Johnson," *NQ*, II (Ser. 9; July 9, 1898), 33-34. A Greek passage. See items 411, 412, 436, and 555.

555.   ———. "Reply to Maxwell," *NQ*, I (Ser. 9; May 21, 1898), 409-410. See items 411, 412, 436, and 554.

556.   SAINTSBURY, George. "Johnson, Boswell, and Goldsmith," *The Peace of the Augustans*, pp. 177-212. London: George Bell and Sons, 1916.

557.   ———. "Some Great Biographies," *Essays in English Literature, 1875-1920*, pp. 412-416. London: J. M. Dent, 1923.

558.   SALPETER, Harry. *Dr. Johnson and Mr. Boswell.* New York: Coward-McCann, 1929. See especially pp. 1-77.

559.   SANDWELL, B. K. "Boswell Performs Boswell," *Saturday Night* (Canada), LXVI (Feb. 13, 1951), 7.

560.   ———. "Things that Bothered Boswell," *Saturday Night* (Canada), LXVII (May 17, 1952), 4-5.

560.1.   SCHALIT, Ann E. "Literature as Product and Process: Two Differing Accounts of the Same Trip," *Serif*, IV (1967), 10-17. Concerns *Hebrides*.

561.   SCHINZ, Albert. "Documents Nouveaux sur Rousseau et Voltaire," *Revue de Paris*, XL (May 15, 1933), 299-325; (June 1, 1933), 630-667. Descriptions of the French philosophers in Boswell's journals and some of his correspondence with them.

562.   SCIOLUS. [J. B. Blakeway] "To James Boswell, Esq.," *Gentleman's Mag.*, LXII (Feb., 1792), 104; (March, 1792), 213-214. Critiques on Vol. II of the first edition of the *Life*.

562.1.   SCRUTATOR. "Boswell Vindicated," *Gentleman's*

Mag., LXIV (March, 1794), 198-199. Comments on the second edition of the *Life*.

562.2. Σεαυτόν, Αἰσχυνεο . *Gentleman's Mag.*, LXIV (Feb., 1794), 120-121. The Seward controversy.

563. SENEX [Horatio Townsend]. "A Blank in Boswell's Journal," *NQ*, CLXXVII (Oct. 28, 1939), 319-320. Reply to item 474.

564. SERGEANT, Philip W. *Liars and Fakers*, pp. 254-255. London: Hutchinson and Co., 1925. Boswell and Samuel Ireland.

565. SEWALL, Richard B. "Rousseau's Second Discourse in England and Scotland from 1762 to 1772," *PQ*, XVIII (1939), 225-242. Pp. 230-237 are especially concerned with Rousseau's influence on Boswell.

565.1. SEWARD, Anna. "Answer to Mr. Boswell," *Gentleman's Mag.*, LXIII (Dec., 1793), 1098-1101. Miss Seward's part in the controversy with Boswell.

565.2. ————. "Boswell's *Johnson*," *Gentleman's Mag.*, LXIII (Oct., 1793), 875. Controversy with Boswell.

566. SHELDON, E. N. "Boswell's English in the London Journal," *PMLA*, LXXI (1956), 1067-1093.

567. SHELTON, F. W. "Boswell: The Biographer," *Knickerbocker Mag.*, XXXVII (Feb., 1851), 153-159. A defense of Boswell and his works.

568. SHERMAN, Stuart. "Boswell on His Own Hook," *Critical Woodcuts*, pp. 271-283. New York: Charles Scribner's Sons, 1926. Boswell's letters.

569.   SHEPHERD, Richard H. "Notes on John Wilkes and
        Boswell's Life of Johnson," *Walford's Antiquar-
        ian*, XI (Jan., 1887), 34-37.

570.   SHERBO, Arthur. "Gleanings from Boswell's 'Note-
        book,'" *NQ*, CCI (March, 1956), 108-112. Self-
        revelations.

570.1. "Short Account of James Boswell, Esq.," *The Aber-
        deen Mag.*, I (Nov., 1796), 266-268. A memoir.

570.2. SHORT, Bob. "Two Allusions to Boswell," *Gentle-
        man's Mag.*, LXIII (June, 1793), 499. Concerns
        the second edition of the *Life*.

571.   SHUCKBURGH, E. S. "'Corsica' Boswell," *Macmil-
        lan's Mag.*, LVI (Oct., 1892), 432-438. Reprinted
        in *Living Age*, CXCV (Dec. 3, 1892), 605-612.
        Boswell in Corsica and after.

572.   SIGMA. "Boswell the Biographer," *NQ*, VI (Ser. 7;
        Nov. 10, 1888), 368. See item 552 for reply.

573.   SILLARD, P. A. "Prince of Biographers," *Atlantic Mo.*,
        LXXXVIII (Aug., 1901), 213-221. A character
        analysis.

574.   SIMPSON, T. B. "Boswell as an Advocate," *Juridical
        Rev.*, XXXIV (1922), 201-225. History of Bos-
        well's legal career.

575.   _____. "Letters of James Boswell," *Fortnightly
        Rev.*, CXXVII (March, 1927), 376-389. Bos-
        well's frankness in his correspondence.

576.   SKRINE, Francis H. "The Johnson Circle: Goldsmith,
        Percy, Boswell, Davies...," *Gossip about Dr.
        Johnson and Others, Being Chapters from the
        Memoirs of Laetitia M. Hawkins*, pp. 126-131.
        London: Eveleigh, Mash and Grayson, 1926.

576.1. SMITH, D. N. *Johnsonians and Boswellians.* Lichfield Johnson Society, 1950.

577. SMITH, Minna Steele. "Manuscript Notes by Madame Piozzi in a Copy of Boswell's 'Life of Johnson,'" *London Mercury*, V (Jan., 1922), 286-293. Reprinted in *Living Age*, CCCXII (March 4, 1922), 536-542.

578. SMITH-DAMPIER, John L. *Who's Who in Boswell?* Oxford University Press, 1935. Identifies names in the *Life*.

579. SPALDING, P. A. *Self-Harvest: Study of Diaries and the Diarist*, pp. 36-38; 84-87. London: Independent Press, Ltd., 1949.

580. STARRETT, Vincent. "Boswell and Dr. Johnson," *Books and Bipeds*, pp. 200-202. New York: Argus Books, 1947.

581. STAUFFER, Donald A. *The Art of Biography in Eighteenth Century England.* Princeton University Press, 1941. Random references to Boswell.

582. STEPHEN, Sir Leslie. "James Boswell," *Dictionary of National Biography*, V (1886), 431-438.

583. STEPHEN, Leslie. "Johnsoniana," *National Rev.*, XXX (Sept., 1897), 61-76. Reprinted with a reply to Fitzgerald (Item 274) in *Studies of a Biographer*, I, 105-146. 4 vols. London: Duckworth and Co., 1898.

584. STEVENSON, Francis Seymour. *Historic Personality*, pp. 24-28, 85-89. London and New York: Macmillan and Co., 1893.

585. STEVENSON, Robert. "'The Rivals'—Hawkins, Burney, and Boswell," *Musical Quarterly*, XXXVI (Jan., 1950), 67-82. Defends Hawkins.

585.1. STEWART, Mary M. "Boswell and the Infidels," *SEL*, IV (1964), 475-483. The religion of Boswell and Gibbon.

586. ————. "Boswell's Denominational Dilemma," *PMLA*, LXXVI (Dec., 1961), 503-511. An outline of Boswell's religious life.

586.1. ————. "James Boswell and the National Church of Scotland," *HLQ*, XXX (1967), 369-387. Boswell in a theological debate.

586.2. ————. "James Hervey's Influence on Boswell," *American NQ*, IV (1966), 117-120.

587. STOBART, M. A. "Boswell in Corsica: The Perfect Journalist on His Travels," *Pall Mall Mag.*, XXV (Oct., 1901), 225-235. A full account.

587.1. STOCHHOLM, J. M. *Garrick's Folly: The Shakespeare Jubilee of 1769 at Stratford and Drury Lane.* New York: Barnes and Noble, 1964. Concerns *Corsica*. See Stochholm's index for references to Boswell.

588. STRACHEY, Lytton. *Biographical Essays*, pp. 147-152. New York: Harcourt, Brace and Co., 1949. Condemns Boswell's moral conduct.

589. ————. "James Boswell," *New Republic*, XLI (Feb. 4, 1925), 283-285. Refers to Tinker as a prude and to Boswell as a lecher. See item 182 and 308.

590. ————. "James Boswell," *Portraits in Miniature*, pp. 86-95. New York: Harcourt, Brace and Co., 1931. Reprint of item 589.

591. ————. "James Boswell," *Modern Short Bio-*

> *graphies*, pp. 94-99. New York: Harcourt, Brace and Co., 1935.

592.   STUCLEY, Elizabeth F. *A Hebridean Journey with Johnson and Boswell*. London: Christopher Johnson, 1956.

593.   TAYLOR, F. "Johnsoniana from the Bagshawe Muniments in the John Rylands Library: Sir James Caldwell, Dr. Hawkesworth, Dr. Johnson, and Boswell's Use of the 'Caldwell Minute,'" *John Rylands Library Bulletin*, XXXV (Sept., 1952), 211-247. Boswell's source for a note in the *Life*.

594.   TAYLOR, John. *Records of My Life*, pp. 126-127. 2 vols. New York: J. And J. Harper, 1833.

595.   THAYER, William Roscoe. *The Art of Biography*, pp. 87-100. New York: Charles Scribner's Sons, 1920. A full account of Boswell's biographical prowess.

596.   ―――――. "Biography in the Nineteenth Century," *NAR*, CCXI (1920), 632-640, 826-833. Boswell's *Life* served as a model.

597.   THOMPSON, Karl F. "An Anonymous 'Epistle to James Boswell,'" *NQ*, CXCIV (1949), 162-163. Asks who was the author, Peter Pindar or Boswell. See item 258.

598.   THORNBURY, Walter. "Boswell and the Keeper of Newgate," *NQ*, VIII (Ser. 4; Nov. 4, 1871), 389. Refers to the Hackman case. See items 211 and 599.

599.   ―――――. "Boswell's Life of Johnson," *NQ*, VII (Ser. 4; June 24, 1871), 532. An error in the *Life*. See items 211 and 598.

600.   "Thoughts on Family and Friends. Some Little-known

Anecdotes and Random Reflections by James Boswell," *Bookman's Journal*, XII (May, 1925), 37-46. A reprint of 423.

600.1. TILLINGHAST, Anthony J. "Boswell Playing a Part," *Renaissance and Modern Studies*, IX (1965), 86-97.

600.2. _____. "The Moral and Philosophical Basis of Johnson's and Boswell's Idea of Biography," *Johnsonian Studies, Including a Bibliography of Johnsonian Studies, 1950-1960*, compiled by J. L. Clifford and Donald J. Greene, pp. 115-131. Cairo: S. O. P. Press, 1963.

600.3. TINKER, Chauncey Brewster. "Boswell and the Art of Intimate Biography," *The Salon and English Letters*, pp. 268-284. New York: Macmillan, 1915.

601. _____. "Boswell in Love," *Atlantic Mo.*, CXXIX (Jan., 1922), 22-29. Boswell and Zélide.

602. _____. "Boswell Takes a Wife," *Atlantic Mo.*, CXXIX (Feb., 1922), 157-166. Boswell, Kate Blair, Margaret Montgomery, and "La Belle Irlandaise."

603. _____. "The Great Diarist, and Some Others," *Essays in Retrospect*, pp. 16-18. New Haven: Yale University Press, 1948. Compares Pepys and Boswell.

604. _____. "Magnum Opus: Boswell's Method in Biography," *Atlantic Mo.*, CXXIX (March, 1922) 356-361. How Boswell contrived the scenes in the *Life*.

605. _____. *Nature's Simple Plan*, pp. 1-77, *et passim*. Princeton University Press; Oxford Univer-

sity Press, 1922. See especially pp. 48-52. Boswell and Corsica.

606. _____. "New Chapter of Boswell; Unpublished Letters to Rousseau and Voltaire," *Atlantic Mo.*, CXXVII (May, 1921), 577-583. Boswell in France. See item 628.

607. _____, and F. A. Pottle. *A New Portrait of James Boswell*. Harvard University Press, 1927.

608. TINKER, Harold Lauren (comp.). "Letter to J. J. Rousseau," *Essays—Yesterday and Today*, pp. 73-78. New York: Macmillan Co., 1934.

609. TODD, William B. "Cowper's Commentary on 'The Life of Johnson,'" *TLS*, March 15, 1957, p. 168. Annotations of the *Life*.

610. TOGAWA, Shukotsu. "Boswell's *Life of Dr. Johnson* as the Theme of Biographical Study," *Studies in English Literature by the English Literary Society of Japan*, XIX (1939), 1-11.

610.1. "To James Boswell, Esq.," *London Mag.*, IV (New ser.; May, 1785), 353. A poem to Boswell.

611. TORRE, Lillian de la. *The Heir of Douglas*, pp. 197-229, *et passim*. New York: Alfred A. Knopf, 1952. Boswell and the Douglas Case, 1767-1769.

612. TRAILL, H. D. "Revolution in Grubstreet: A Boswellian Fragment," *Fortnightly Rev.*, LXIV (New series LVIII (July, 1895), 78-88. An undocumented piece on Edward Dilly.

613. TUCKER, William J. "Prince of Biographers," *Catholic World*, CLXIII (June, 1946), 218-224. Defends Boswell.

614.   VERAX. *Remarks on the Journal of a Tour to the He-*
         brides. In a Letter to J. Boswell, Esq. London:
         Printed for J. Debrett, opposite Burlington
         House, In Piccadilly, 1785. See item 354.

615.   VEROSKY, Sister M. Victorine. "John Walker's One
         Clergyman," *NQ*, CCVI (1961), 126-128.

615.1.   VIGORNIENSIS. "Origin of the Word Tontine," *Gen-*
         tleman's mag., LX (Supplement. 1790), 1194.
         Concerns *Corsica.*

616.   VULLIAMY, C. E. *Ursa Major: A Study of Dr. Johnson*
         and His Friends. London: Michael Joseph, 1946.
         See especially pp. 64-86, 257-267, and 296-314.

617.   "Vulliamy's Boswell," *Nation*, CXXXVI (April 5,
         1933), 377. Comments on item 41.

617.1.   W., T. "Burial Service," *Gentleman's Mag.*, LXIV
         (July, 1794), 620. Comments on the *Life.*

618.   WALCUTT, Charles C. "Captain Marryat and Bos-
         well's 'Life of Johnson,'" *NQ*, CLXXIV (Jan. 8,
         1938), 27-28. Borrowings from Boswell's *Life.*

619.   WALKER, Hugh. "Wise Men Who Have Passed for
         Fools," *Yale Rev.*, V (1916), 587-604. Includes
         Boswell.

620.   WALKER, R. J. "James Boswell, Inquiring Reporter,"
         Hobbies, LIX (Nov. 4, 1954), 133; 147.

621.   WALLER, John F. *Boswell and Johnson: Their Com-*
         panions and Contemporaries. London: Cassell
         and Co., 1881.

622.   WALTHEOF. "Boswell," *NQ*, VIII (Ser. 4; Dec. 30,
         1871), 557. See items 151 and 154.

623. WARD, C. A. "Boswell," *NQ*, IV (Ser. 5; Nov. 6, 1875), 376. Boswell's London dwellings. See items 142 and 377.

624. WARNOCK, Robert. "Boswell and Andrew Lumisden," *MLQ*, II (1941), 601-607.

625. _____. "Boswell and Bishop Trail," *NQ*, CLXX-IV (Jan. 15, 1938), 44-45. Their meeting in Florence.

626. _____. "Boswell on the Grand Tour," *SP*, XXX-IX (1942), 650-661. Boswell in Italy.

627. _____. "Boswell and Some Italian Literati," *Interchange Fortnightly*, I (1940), 82-83.

628. _____. "Boswell and Wilkes in Italy," *ELH*, III (1936), 257-269. A record of their association. See item 606.

629. _____. "Nuove Lettere Inedite di Giuseppe Baretti," *Giornale Storica della Literatura Italiana*, CXXXI (1954), 73-87. Boswell-Baretti correspondence.

630. WATSON, Melvin R. " 'Momus' and Boswell's *Tour*," *JEGP*, XLVIII (1949), 371-374. Concerns an early critic of Boswell's *Hebrides*.

631. WATTS, Henry, "Boswell: Was he a Catholic?" *America*, LVI (1936), 186-187. See item 466.

632. WECTER, Dixon. "Dr. Johnson, Mrs. Thrale, and Boswell: Three Letters," *MLN*, LVI (1941), 525-529. Unpublished correspondence.

633. _____. "Four Unpublished Letters from Boswell to Burke," *MP*, XXXVI (1938), 47-58. Boswell's efforts to make Burke's acquaintance.

634.   _____. "The Soul of James Boswell," *VQR*, XII (1936), 195-206. Boswell's interest in Catholicism.

635.   WELLS, Mitchell. "James Boswell and the Modern Dilemma," *SAQ*, XLVIII (1949), 432-441. Boswell's religious problems.

636.   WERKMEISTER, Lucyle. "Jemmie Boswell and the London Daily Press, 1785-1795," *BNYPL*, LXVII (Feb., 1963), 82-114; (March, 1963), 169-185. Boswell's contributions of Johnsoniana and other materials to London newspapers during the period.

637.   _____. *The London Daily Press, 1772-1792*. Lincoln: University of Nebraska Press, 1963.

638.   "When Boswell Dared to Differ," *TLS*, Jan. 9, 1919, pp. 13-14.

639.   WHIBLEY, Leonard. "Boswell's Journals," *Blackwood's Mag.*, CCXIII (March, 1923), 395-406. History and compilation of the journals.

640.   _____. "Boswell Without Johnson," *Blackwood's Mag.*, CCXVII (Feb., 1925), 250-270. Boswell as seen through his letters.

640.1.   WHITE, Henry. "Seward and Boswell," *Gentleman's Mag.*, LXIV (March, 1794), 196-197. The controversy with Anna Seward.

641.   "Whoever Will Write a Life," *Public Opinion*, May 10, 1912, p. 452.

642.   WHYTE, E. A. "Remarks on Boswell's Life of Johnson," *A Miscellany*, pp. 1-42. Dublin: E. A. and S. Whyte, 1799. Re-issued as *Miscellanea Nova*.

Dublin: Robert Marchbank for E. A. and S. Whyte, 1801.

642.1.   WILLIAM. *Gentleman's Mag.*, LXVII (Feb., 1797), 104. Identifies the author of item 124.

643.   WILLING- DENTON, E. K. "Boswell and the Copyright of the *Life*," *TLS*, Dec. 1, 1932, p. 923. See item 339.

644.   _____. "Piozzian Rhymes," *TLS*, April 20, 1933, p. 276. Reply to item 285.

645.   WILSON, Edmund. "Boswell and Others," *New Repub.*, XLIII (July 1, 1925), 153-154. Condemns Boswell as one more poor product of the Eighteenth Century.

645.1.   WIMSATT, W. K. "The Fact Imagined: James Boswell," *Hateful Contraries: Studies in Literature and Criticism*, pp. 165-183. Lexington: University of Kentucky Press, 1966.

646.   _____. "Foote and a Friend of Boswell's: A Note on the *Nabob*," *MLN*, LVII (May, 1942), 325-335

647.   _____. "James Boswell: The Man and the Journal," *Yale Rev.*, XLIX (Sept., 1959), 80-92. Boswell's technique in *London Journal*.

648.   WINDLE, Bertram C. A. "Bozzy," *Catholic World*, CXXV (July, 1927), 433-442. Boswell is responsible for much of Johnson's modern fame.

649.   WOOLF, Virginia. "Mrs. Thrale," *New Statesman and Nation*, XXI (March 8, 1941), 250. Random comments on Boswell.

649.1.   X., L. *Gentleman's Mag.*, LXIV (March, 1794), 220. Comments on the *Life*.

649.2.   XIMENES. "Boswell's *Letter to the People of Scotland, 1785,*" *Gentleman's Mag.*, LV (Sept., 1785), 680-682.

649.3.   Y., N. "Mr. Boswell and Miss Seward," *Gentleman's Mag.*, LXIV (Jan., 1794), 7. The controversy with Anna Seward.

650.   YOKLAVICH, J. "Hamlet in Shammy Shoes," *Shakespeare Quarterly*, III (July, 1952), 209-218.

651.   YOUNG, George M. "Boswell—and Unashamed," *Daylight and Champaign; Essays*, pp. 260-263. London: Rupert Hart-Davis, 1948.

651.1.   Z. "Sir Joshua Reynolds," *Gentleman's Mag.*, LXII (Supplement, 1792), 1200.

652.   Z., A. "Remarks on Boswell's *Life,*" *Gentleman's Mag.*, LXI (June, 1791), 533-534. A critique of details.

SECTION FIVE
Theses and Dissertations

Section Five
Theses and Dissertations

653.   ANSDELL, Ora Joye. "Boswell of Scotland: The Importance of the Years Among Hid Countrymen in Developing His Character." University of Colorado, 1956.

654.   BENNETT, Charles H. "Letters Between the Honourable Andrew Erskine and James Boswell, Esq." Yale University, 1932.

655.   BINGHAM, Sylvester H. "Publishing in the Eighteenth Century, with Special Reference to the Firm of Edward and Charles Dilly." Yale University, 1937.

656.   BRADY, Frank. "The Political Career of James Boswell." Yale University, 1952. See item 159.1.

657.   BROOKS, Alfred R. "The Literary and Intellectual Foundations of James Boswell." University of Wisconsin, 1957. See item 163.

657.1.   BROWN, Anthony E. "The Literary Reputation of James Boswell to 1785." Vanderbilt University, 1971.

658.   BURKE, Mary D. "Selected Correspondence of James Boswell, 1770-1773." Yale University, 1955.

659.   COLE, Richard C. "The Correspondence of James Boswell in 1769." Yale University, 1955.

660.   DIXON, Arthur W. "The Correspondence of James Boswell and His Sons, Alexander and James." Yale University, 1953.

661.   FIFER, Charles N. "Letters Between James Boswell and Six Members of the Club." Yale University, 1954.

662.   FOLADARE, Joseph. "James Boswell and Corsica." Yale University, 1936.

662.1. HANKINS, J. D. "Early Correspondence of James Boswell, 1757-1766." Indiana University, 1964.

663.   HANKINS, Nellie Pottle. "The Correspondence of James Boswell and James Bruce." University of Kansas, 1959.

664.   LANG, Daniel. "Dr. Samuel Johnson in America; A Study of His Reputation, 1750-1812." University of Illinois, 1939.

665.   LINCOLN, Eleanor T. "James Boswell, Reader and Critic." Yale University, 1938.

665.1. LUSTIG, Irma S. "Boswell's Portrait of Himself in *The Life of Samuel Johnson*." University of Pennsylvania, 1963.

666.   MILD, Warren P. "Macaulay as a Critic of Eighteenth Century English Literature." University of Minnesota, 1951.

667.   MURRAY, John. "James Boswell in Edinburgh." Yale University, 1939.

667.1. PALMER, Joyce A. C. "Boswell's *Life of Johnson* as Literary History." University of Tennessee, 1967.

667.2. POTTLE, Frederick A. "The Literary Career of James Boswell to 1785." Yale University, 1925.

668.   PROBSTEIN, Inge. "Boswell's London Journal, 1778." Yale University, 1952.

THESES AND DISSERTATIONS

669. ROBERTSON, James D. "The Opinions of the Eighteenth Century Men of Letters Concerning Scotland." University of Cincinnati, N. D.

670. SAUNDERS, Alexander M. "In Search of the Landscape; English Travels in the British Isles from 1760-1810." Johns Hopkins University, 1941.

671. WAINGROW, Marshall. "Five Correspondences of James Boswell Relating to the Composition of *The Life of Johnson.*" Yale University, 1951.

672. WARNOCK, Robert. "Boswell in Italy." Yale University, 1932. See item 6.

673. WAHBURN, John Lawrence. "Boswell's Roles." Honors Thesis. Harvard University, 1959.

674. WEIS, Charles McC. "The Correspondence of James Boswell and Sir David Dalrymple (Lord Hailes)." Yale University, 1954.

ADDENDA

Addenda

Note: The following list of 18th Century materials on Boswell and his
work was compiled during the summer of 1971, when the main
work was already in press. The sheer amount of the contemporary
commentary and the surprising information contained in some of
the items have warranted this supplemental list.

For the sake of what I hope will be clarity, I have keyed the new
material with the numbers of the items in the original list without
adding extra decimals or letters to the new items. The user of the
book should be aware, then, that item number 95 in this supplement (*Aberdeen Mag.*, I (Jan., 1761), 54) alphabetically follows
immediately after item number 95 in the "General Studies" section
of the main list.

I was able to compile these addenda with the aid of a grant from
the American Philosophical Society and through the kindnesses of
the librarians of the Sterling Memorial Library and the Beinecke
Rare Book Library at Yale University.

A. E. B.

Editions

7.   Reviews of Corsica: *The Court Miscellany, or Gen-
tleman and Lady's New Mag.*, IV (Feb., 1768),
61-66; (March, 1768), 143-148; (April, 1768), 191-
196. (Extracts only); *Lloyd's Evening Post*, XXII
(Feb. 12-15, 1768), 156; (Feb. 15-17, 1768), 164;
(Feb. 17-19, 1768), 172; (May 25-27, 1768), 508;
(June 13-15, 1768), 572; (June 20-22, 1768), 599.
(P. 599 has the only critical comment); *Political
Register*, II (April, 1768), 320.

12.   Advertisements of *Tour to the Hebrides: Edinburgh
Advertiser*, XLIV (Oct. 11, 1785), 237; *Edinburgh
Evening Courant*, Oct. 1, 1785, p. 1, col. 2; Oct.
8, 1785, p. 1, col. 1; Oct. 10, 1785, p. 1, col. 1;
London Chronicle, LVIII (Sept. 10-13, 1785),

255; (Sept. 17-20, 1785), 279; (Sept. 24-27, 1785), 300; *St. James's Chronicle*, Sept. 10-13, 1785, p. 3, col. 4; Sept. 22-24, 1785, p. 3, col. 4. Second Edition Advertisements: *General Evening Post*, Dec. 20-22, 1785, p. 4, col. 4; *London Chronicle*, LVIII (Dec. 13-15, 1785), 574; (Dec. 22-24, 1785), 603.

Reviews of *Tour to the Hebrides*: *St. James's Chronicle*, Oct. 4-6, 1785, p. 2, col. 1; *Westminster Mag.*, XIII (Oct., 1785), 537-541; (Nov., 1785), 582-585.

Extracts of the Prince Charles Edward account from the *Tour to the Hebrides*: (Note: The titles vary somewhat) *Edinburgh Evening Courant*, Oct. 12, 1785, p. 2, cols. 1-2; Oct. 17, 1785, p. 1, cols. 1-2; p. 2, col. 1; *General Evening Post*, Oct. 13-15, 1785, p. 2, cols. 2-4; Oct. 15-18 (misprinted 17 in the *Post*), 1785, p. 2, cols. 1-2; Oct. 20-22, 1785, p. 3, cols. 2-3; *London Chronicle*, LVIII (Oct. 20-22, 1785), 385-386; (Oct. 22-25, 1785), 393; (Oct. 25-27, 1785), 401.

20.   Review of *Dorando*: *Political Register*, I (July, 1767), 179.

20.   Reprinted as "The Prince of Dorando: A Spanish Tale," *The New Town and Country Mag.*, II (May, 1788), 233-237; (June, 1788), 309-312. Reprints 90% of Boswell's text, with many changes in capitalization, punctuation, and spelling. Boswell's text becomes increasingly altered (through omissions) as each of the two installments approaches the end of the space apparently allotted it.

21.   "Publications Announced," *Essays Reflecting Men and Manners. By the Late James Boswell, Esq.* Published originally in the *London Magazine*, and now first collected into one volume, large 8vo. By Mr. John Lawrie, Clerk and private sec-

retary to Mr. Boswell, and Principal Clerk to the late Sir James Stewart, Bart. Authour of Political Economy. *Monthly Epitome*, III (Sept., 1799), 356. Lawrie's plan was apparently stopped before publication could begin, for there is no further notice of the *Essays*.

29.   Advertisements of the *Life: Edinburgh Advertiser*, LV (May 27, 1791), 335; *London Chronicle*, LXVII (Jan. 21-23, 1790), 75; LXIX (March 15-17, 1791), 262; (April 28-30, 1791), 413; (May 5-7, 1791), 437; *St. James's Chronicle*, Sept. 16-18, 1790, p. 4, col. 3; March 17-19, 1791, p. 4, col. 2; May 12-14, 1791, p. 3, col. 4.

Reviews of 1st edition of the *Life: Analytical Rev.*, X (July, 1791), 241-250; (Appendix, 1791), 481-489; XI (Dec., 1791), 361-376; *Historical Mag.*, III (June, 1791), 167-172; (July, 1791), 257-259; (Aug., 1791), 297-300; (Sept., 1791), 325-329; (Oct., 1791), 369-375; (Nov., 1791), 399-405; (Dec., 1791), 438-444 (P. 167 has the only critical comment); *Literary Mag. and British Rev.*, VIII (Jan., 1792), 52-58; (April, 1792), 293-296; (May, 1792), 376-378; IX (July, 1792), 63-68; (August, 1792), 148-152; *St. James's Chronicle*, May 14-17, 1791, p. 4, cols. 1-2.

Reviews of 3rd edition of the *Life: Monthly Mirror*, VIII (Sept., 1799), 154; *Monthly Epitome*, III (May, 1799), 191 (Notice only).

General Studies

95.   *Aberdeen Mag.*, I (Jan., 1761), 54. Notice of *Observations on "The Minor."*

95.1.   "Account of the Jubilee at Stratford-upon-Avon," *Court Miscellany*, V (Sept., 1769), 439-443. A reprint of Boswell's account.

97.   "Addressed to James B——s——ll, Esq.," *St.*

James's Chronicle, Dec. 2-4, 1790, p. 4, col. 1. (Poets Corner) Two parodies of Boswell's poetic praises of Mrs. Jordan, actress.

99. "Anecdote of Dr. Johnson," *St. James's Chronicle*, May 21-23, 1791, p. 4, col. 1. Boswell on Johnson's ambition.

99. "Anecdote of G. Faulkner and Dr. Johnson," *London Chronicle*, LVIII (Oct. 1-4, 1785), 323. Their conversation on the poor people of Ireland.

99. "Anecdotes of the Illustrious Corsican Chief, Signior Pascal Paoli. Extracted from Mr. Boswell's Tour to Corsica," *Court Miscellany*, V (July, 1769), 338-343. With an engraving of Paoli.

101.2. B., A. "To the Editor," *Political Register*, II (Extraordinary Issue, 1768), 193-202. P. 197 concerns *Corsica*.

123. "Biographical Sketch of Mrs. Piozzi," *Monthly Mirror*, V (June, 1798), 323-325; VI (Sept., 1798), 137-138. Random comment on Boswell as biographer.

139.1. Boswell, James. "General Paoli," *St. James's Chronicle*, Dec. 25-28, 1790, p. 2, cols. 1-2. Boswell prints and comments on Paoli's speech to the General Assembly of Corsica.

148.3. "Boswell's Version of Johnsoniana," *General Evening Post*, Sept. 29-Oct. 1, 1785, p. 1, col. 2; Oct. 1-4, 1785, p. 3, col. 2; Oct. 6-8, 1785, p. 3, col. 3; Oct. 8-11, 1785, p. 3, cols. 2-3; Oct. 29-Nov. 1, 1785, p. 3, col. 3; Nov. 1-3, 1785, p. 3, col. 2. Extracts from *Hebrides*.

174.1. C., A. B. "To the biographical Historian of Sir William Blackstone," *St. James's Chronicle*, Oct. 25-27,

1785, p. 1, col. 2. Boswell on Johnson and Gold-smith.

187. CAUSIDICUS. "A Poetical Epistle to James Boswell, Esq. On his Life of Dr. Johnson," *St. James's Chronicle*, June 7-9, 1791, p. 4, col. 1. (Poets Corner); reprinted by "C" in *Public Advertiser*, June 10, 1791.

188. Add to item 188: "Lesson in Biography," *Lady's Mag.*, XXII (July, 1791), 370-373; reprinted as "Modern Biography, extracted from the Life of Dr. Pozz, in ten Volumes Folio, written by James Bozz, Esq, who flourished with him near fifty Years," *Town and Country Mag.*, XXIII (July, 1791), 318-320. This piece originally appeared in the *Morning Herald*, July 5, 1791, and in the *Public Advertiser*, July 6, 1791.

209. "Character of the late Dr. Johnson. By James Boswell, Esq.," *General Evening Post*, Oct. 4-6, 1785, p. 3, cols. 2-3; also in *London Chronicle*, LVIII (Oct. 8-11, 1785), 349.

224. "County of Ayr," *Edinburgh Advertiser*, XLIV (Sept. 20, 1785), 190. Lists Boswell as a member of the "General Association for the PRESERVATION of GAME in this County."

224. "County of Ayr," *Edinburgh Advertiser*, XLIV (Oct. 28, 1785), 276; reprinted as "County of Ayr Meeting," *Edinburgh Evening Courant*, Oct. 29, 1785, p. 2, cols. 2-3. Boswell's activities concerning the Court of Session.

230. "Curious Anecdote of Dr. Johnson. From Boswell's Life of the Doctor." *Bon Ton Mag.*, I (June, 1791), 143. Concerns Beauclerk and Mme. de Boufflers.

238.   "Dialogue of the Dead. A Fragment," *The Spirit of the Public Journals*, II (1798), 116-123. An imaginary conversation, parodying the *Life*.

240.   "Dr. Dodd," *London Chronicle*, LXIX (June 9-11, 1791), 555. Letters between Johnson and Dodd quoted from the *Life*.

240.1. "Dr. Johnson," *Monthly Mirror*, XIV (Oct., 1802), 229-231. Points out an omission from the *Life*.

240.1. "Dr. Johnson," *St. James's Chronicle*, May 28-31, 1791, p. 4, col. 1. Comments on Johnson's comparison of "Scoundrel" and "Whig."

255.   *Edinburgh Advertiser*, LVI (July 12, 1791), 25. Anecdote of "Leveling" quoted from the *Life*.

255.   "Edinburgh Effluvia, upon Scotch Evidence," *St. James's Chronicle*, Sept. 29-Oct. 1, 1785, p. 4, col. 1. Boswell's "I smell you in the dark" passage from *Hebrides* compared with another account of sewerage problems.

255.   *Edinburgh Evening Courant*, June 4, 1785, p. 1, col. 1. Comments on Boswell's 1785 *Letter to the People. . .*

257.   An Enemy to Nonsense and Slander [Edmond Malone]. *St. James's Chronicle*, Oct. 6-8, 1785, p. 4, col. 1. Boswell and *Hebrides* defended.

257.   "Epigram," *St. James's Chronicle*, Feb. 24-26, 1785, p. 4, col. 1. (Poets Corner). A poem on all Johnson's biographers.

262.   "Extract from a Cancelled Sheet of Boswell's Life of Johnson," *The Spirit of the Public Journals*, V (1801), 368-369. A parody on the *Life*.

ADDENDA

262. "Extract from the Memoirs of *The Life of The Orang Outang*," *The Spirit of the Public Journals*, II (1798), 153-157. Johnson depicted as a monkey.

263.1. FERGUSSON, Sir James. "Boswell's First Flame," *Scots Mag.*, New Ser. XIX (Aug., 1933), 331-334.

297. *General Evening Post*, Oct. 1-4, 1785, p. 4, col. 3. An extract from *Hebrides* concerning St. Andrews University.

298. "Gleanings from Boswell's Life of Dr. Johnson," *Lady's Mag.*, XXII (May, 1791), 227-231; (June, 1791), 295-299; (July, 1791), 351-356; (Sept., 1791), 480-483. All extracts.

352. "James Boswell," *Universal Mag.*, XCVI (June, 1795), 399-400. A brief comment on Boswell's character.

358. "Johnsoniana," *St. James's Chronicle*, Dec. 13-15, 1785, p. 4, col. 1. (Poets Corner). Warns authors about such biographers as Boswell.

358. "Johnsoniana; not in Boswell," *The Spirit of the Public Journals*, I (1797), 197-198. On Johnson's conversation.

368. Add to 368: *Analytical Rev.*, VII (July, 1790), 303-304. A review of Kenrick's *Epistle*, praising Boswell.

382. "A Letter from Dr. Samuel Johnson in the Shades, to his Biographers," *Westminster Mag.*, XIII (April, 1785), 178-179. Ridicules all of the biographers.

382. *A Letter to James Boswell, Esq., with some Remarks on Johnson's Dictionary and on Language, Etc.* London: Kirby, 1792. Reviewed in *Analytical Rev.*, XIV (Oct., 1792), 232. Advice to Boswell, but there is more on Johnson.

387.   *Lloyd's Evening Post, and British Chronicle,* XXI
         (Dec. 2-4, 1767), 538. Concerns Boswell's edition
         of the *Letters of Lady Jane Douglas.*

388.1.   *London Chronicle,* LVII (Jan. 4-6, 1785), 20. Criticises
         Boswell's efforts to have Johnson's pension in-
         creased.

388.1.   *London Chronicle,* LVII (June 18-21, 1785), 584-585.
         Concerns Boswell's 1785 *Letter to the People. . . .*

391.   A Lover of Extraordinary Extracts. "Johnson and
         Bozzy On Pride of Birth," *St. James's Chronicle,*
         Sept. 22-24, 1791, p. 4, cols. 1-2. A parody of the
         Life.

391.   —————. "Johnson and Bozzy On Power and Pre-
         rogative," *St. James's Chronicle,* Nov. 15-17, 1791,
         p. 2, cols. 1-2. An odd parody, having Boswell
         and Johnson predict the French Revolution.

398.   M. *The Character of Dr. Johnson, with Illustrations
         from Mrs. Piozzi, Sir John Hawkins, and Mr.
         Boswell.* London: Dilly, 1792. Reviewed in
         Analytical Rev., XIII (July, 1792), 272-273. The
         reviewer is disgusted with the eclectic view of
         Johnson that emerges.

398.   M., F. D. "Boswell's Executions, A Query," *TLS,*
         April 13, 1922, p. 244. Boswell and the Hackman
         hanging.

398.   M., M. *St. James's Chronicle,* Oct. 22-25, 1785, p. 1,
         col. 2. Praises the *St. James's* for fair reviews of
         Hebrides.

419.1.   MEMOIRICUS. "Dr. Samuel Johnson," *Carlton-House
         Mag.,* II (Aug., 1793), 287-290; (Dec., 1793), 494-
         495. Paraphrases from the biographers, mainly
         Boswell.

420.   "Memoirs of James Boswell, Esq.," *Walker's Hibernian Mag.*, Aug., 1795, pp. 109-112. A kind sketch.

423.   "Mr. Boswell's Sketch of the Person and Character of Dr. Samuel Johnson," *Walker's Hibernian Mag.*, Nov., 1785, pp. 563-568. Extracts from *Hebrides*.

423.   "Mr. Humdrum's Tour to Scotland. A Burlesque Parody of Mr. Boswell's Account of Dr. Johnson's Tour to the Hebrides," *Walker's Hibernian Mag.*, Dec. 1785, pp. 629-632. One of the better parodies.

425.   "Momus; or the Laughing Philosopher," *Westminster Mag.*, XIII (Nov., 1785), 590-594. A humorous parody of *Hebrides*, with a comment on tours in general.

425.   *Monthly Rev.*, XXIII (Dec., 1760), 524. A notice of *A View of the Edinburgh Theatre*.

431.   *Morning Herald*, May 22, 1795, p. 3, col. 3. Obituary of Boswell.

454.   One Not of "Other Times," *St. James's Chronicle*, Oct. 18-20, 1785, p. 2, cols. 1-2. Defends Boswell's account of Johnson on McPherson.

454.   One of the People, "Dr. Johnson's Politicks," *St. James's Chronicle*, Sept. 15-17, 1791, p. 1, col. 3. A Burkite quotes from Boswell's *Life*.

469.   "Pindar's Bozzy and Piozzi Reviewed," *Walker's Hibernian Mag.*, June, 1785, pp. 311-313.

471.   *The Pocket Mag.*, II (May, 1795), 349. Obituary of Boswell.

472.   *Political Register*, I (Nov., 1767), 463. Comments on the *Essence of the Douglas Cause*.

472. *Political Register*, II (Jan., 1768), 62. Comments on *The Letters of Lady Jane Douglas*.

514. "Presentiment," *St. James's Chronicle*, June 28-30, 1791, p. 4, col. 1. Johnson on ghosts, with a critical footnote.

555. *St. James's Chronicle; or British Evening Post*, Jan. 27-29, 1785, p. 4, col. 1. A letter praising Boswell.

555. —————, April 30-May 3, 1791, p. 1, col. 2. Boswell attended the annual dinner of the Royal Academicians.

555. —————, May 14-17, 1791, p. 4, col. 3. Boswell *the* biographer.

555. —————, May 17-19, 1791, p. 4, col. 1. (Poets Corner). Praises Boswell for publishing Johnson's "Ode: Friendship," in the *Life*.

555. —————, May 17-19, 1791, p. 4, col. 3. Boswell on Malone's Shakespeare.

555. —————, May 21-23, 1791, p. 4, col. 4. Boswell on Savage in the *Life*.

555. —————, May 24-26, 1791, p. 4, col. 3. Boswell's account of Johnson's comparison of "Whig" and "Scoundrel."

555. —————, June 2-4, 1791, p. 4, col. 3. Boswell and Literary Property.

555. —————, June 2-4, 1791, p. 4, col. 3. Boswell's use of Hastings' letters in the *Life*.

555. —————, June 18-21, 1791, p. 2, cols. 1-2. Extract,

with comment, on a Johnson letter to Hastings in the *Life*.

555. —————, Nov. 15-17, 1791, p. 3, col. 3. Boswell elected Secretary for Foreign Correspondence to the Royal Academy.

558. "Samuel Johnson," *St. James's Chronicle*, Jan. 8-11, 1785, p. 4. cols. 1-2. Praises Boswell as *the* biographer of Johnson. Perhaps the writer is George Steevens.

562. *Scottish Register*, VI (April-June, 1795), 356. Obituary of Boswell. Misspells Boswell's address "Great Poland St."

562.1. Search No. 2. "David Hume = James Boswell," *NQ*, VII (Ser. 3; March 11, 1865), 197.

575. "Sketch of the Character of the late James Boswell, Esq.," *Walker's Hibernian Mag.*, June, 1795, 528.

575. "Sketch of the Person and Character of Dr. Johnson, from Mr. Boswell's Tour to the Hebrides, just published," *Edinburgh Advertiser*, XLIV (Oct. 14, 1785), 241.

578. S———n. "Johnsonian Market," *St. James's Chronicle*, July 5-7, 1791, p. 4, col. 1. A satirical comment on Boswell as the last "grocer" of the Johnson "produce."

579. "Specimen of Modern Biography: A Sheet Omitted in a Voluminous Life of Johnson," *The Spirit of the Public Journals*, III (1799), 94-96. A parody of the *Life*.

579. Squib. "Epigram," *St. James's Chronicle*, March 5-8,

1791, p. 4, col. 1. (Poets Corner). Criticises Boswell as a poet and a "puffer."

642. Add to 642: Reviewed in *Analytical Rev.*, XXVI (Nov., 1797), 604. Supports Boswell against Whyte. Also, *The New London Rev.*, III (Feb., 1800), 186-187.

648. WINTER, J. G. "A Point in Boswell's Favor," *Michigan Alumnus*, LVIII (May 24, 1952), 236-246.

651. Z. *Edinburgh Advertiser*, XLIV (Nov. 4, 1785), 289. Questions Boswell concerning the Court of Session judges.

SUBJECT INDEX

Subject
Index

(By entry number. The letter "A" after a number indicates
that the entry is in the Addenda.)

SUBJECT INDEX